ST AUGUSTINE'S CITY OF GOD

ST AUGUSTINE'S CITY OF GOD · A VIEW OF THE CONTENTS · *By* JOSEPH RICKABY, S.J.

WIPF & STOCK · Eugene, Oregon

Wipf and Stock Publishers
199 W 8th Ave, Suite 3
Eugene, OR 97401

St. Augustine's City of God
A View of the Contents
By Rickaby, Joseph, S. J.
ISBN 13: 978-1-60608-383-3
Publication date 12/5/2008
Previously published by Benziger Brothers, 1925

ST AUGUSTINE'S CITY OF GOD

IN A.D. 410 Rome was taken and sacked, not destroyed, by Alaric the Goth. The fall of the Eternal City filled the civilised world with consternation. For a century, since Constantine, the Emperors, except Julian, had been Christian. Paganism had been repressed by law; and though pagans still were numerous, especially in the educated classes, the Empire on the whole wore a fair semblance of a Christian State. Then the catastrophe, long threatened, had come at last. Barbarism had triumphed. Whose fault was it? It was obvious to say that it was all along of Christianity. Century after century there had been of victorious paganism: one century of Christianity had brought decadence and ruin.

To meet this reproach, St Augustine took up his pen in 412, and began the work that we know as *The City of God*. Year by year it grew, filling up such leisure as episcopal administration and polemics allowed. It was like one of those large houses that are built by addition of room to room and block to block, as occasion requires, not without a plan, but on a plan comprehensive and discursive. Indeed, I had almost said that *The City of God* was St Augustine's *scrapbook* for fifteen years, A.D. 412-427. It was originally dedicated to Marcellinus, Imperial Vicar of Africa, who was slain in September, 413 (see St Augustine's Letters 136, 138, 151). By 415 the "books," or main divisions of the work, had grown to five (Letter 169); there were eleven in 416; fourteen in 420; and the whole was finished in 427, the remarkable year in which St Augustine penned his crowning treatise on Predestination, *De correptione et gratia*, three years before his death.

This is St Augustine's own account of the work, in the second book of his Retractations:

Meanwhile Rome was overthrown by a raid of Goths, led by King Alaric, a most destructive invasion. The polytheistic worshippers of false gods, whom we commonly call "pagans,"[1] endeavoured to bring this overthrow home to the Christian religion, and began to blaspheme the true God with unusual sharpness and bitterness. This set me on fire with zeal for the house of God, and I commenced to write the books *Of the City of God* against their blasphemies or errors. This work occupied me for a number of years, owing to numerous interruptions of businesses that would not brook delay and had a prior claim on me. At last this large work *Of the City of God* was brought to a conclusion in twenty-two books. The first five of them are a refutation of their position who maintain that the worship of many gods, according to the custom of paganism, is essential to the prosperity of human society, and that the prohibition of it is the source and origin of calamities such as the fall of Rome. The next five books are against those who, while allowing that such calamities are never wanting, and never will be wanting, to the page of mortal history, and are now great, now small, under varying conditions of place, time, and person, yet argue that polytheistic worship, and sacrifice to many gods, is profitable for the life that follows after death. These first ten books, then, are a refutation of these two vain opinions adverse to the Christian religion. But not to expose ourselves to the reproach of merely having refuted the other side without establishing our own position, we have made that assertion of our own position the object of the second part of this work, which comprises twelve books; though, to be sure, in the former ten, where needful, we vindicate our own, and in the latter twelve we confute the opposite party. Of the twelve following books, four contain the origin of the Two Cities, the one of God, the other of this world. The next four contain the course of their

[1] *Pagan, paganus* (from *pagus*, a *country place*), originally meant *civilian*. It appears that the military class, and all other persons who had employment under Government, were the more amenable to imperial influence exerted in favour of Christianity.

history; the third and last four their several due ends. Thus the whole twenty books, though written of Two Cities, yet take their title from the better of the two, and are entitled by preference *Of the City of God.*

Every great work, in so far as it is a work of man, is open to criticism. This of St Augustine lies open to the criticism that the Two Cities are not organised as cities. The City of this world, called Babylon, "the city of confusion," is not organised at all. There is no one systematic coalition of all bad men against the good. Indeed, it is often hard to distinguish who the bad men are. The bad are by no means bad all over, and there is much evil among the good. In this life there is no *great gulf fixed* (Luke xvi 26) between the good and the bad. St Augustine's dichotomy is too absolute. It may be replied that some men are in the state of sanctifying grace and some are out of it; and that is a great gulf. Again, that some men are elect, others reprobate—again a great gulf. These are gulfs, indeed, but not apparent gulfs; our eyes cannot discern with any certainty the elect from the reprobate, nor see the soul in grace. A city is a visible, organised construction: the elect and reprobate on earth are not thus two cities. The Catholic Church is such a city, a visible organism. But the Catholic Church has existed only for nineteen hundred years, whereas St Augustine dates his City of God from the earliest days of man on earth. His Two Cities, then, cannot be accurately described as the Church and the World. Once more, I say, the World is not an organised body, organised for the damnation of mankind, as the Church is organised for their salvation.

In fact, the Two Cities are not the Church and the World, but the Elect and the Reprobate. This St Augustine lays down clearly:

We distribute the human race into two kinds of men, one living according to man, the other living according to God.

Mystically, we call them Two Cities, or two societies of men: the one of which is predestined to reign eternally with God, the other to suffer eternal punishment with the devil (*C. D.*, xv, 1).

The Elect and the Reprobate do not form two visible societies on earth. To identify the Church on earth with the Elect would be a gross piece of Jansenism, such as Clement XI, in his Bull *Unigenitus*, condemned in condemning the following propositions of Paschal Quesnel—No. 72: "It is a note of the Christian Church that it is Catholic, comprising at once all the angels of heaven, and all the elect and just of earth, and of all ages." No. 74: "The Church, or the whole Christ, has the Word Incarnate for Head, and all the saints as members." No. 76: "Nothing more roomy than the Church of God, because all the elect and righteous of all ages compose it."

Nothing could be more anti-Augustinian than such teaching. The cardinal point that St Augustine continually pressed against the Donatists was precisely this, that elect and reprobate live side by side and together make up the Church on earth, the Church being the net of the parable (Matt. xiii 47-8) taking *fishes good and bad.*

Consider St Augustine himself in the days of his sinful youth, which he has recorded in his *Confessions.* He was certainly one of the Elect, but to which City did he belong in those days, to Babylon or to Jerusalem? At this hour there are many of the Elect living like reprobates: there are doubtless also reprobates living at present the life of the Elect. To which City do they severally belong? These Two Cities are blended together in this world, till they are parted at the Last Judgement (*C. D.*, i, 35).

The Catholic Church, indeed, stands as a city on a mountain, distinct and clear in its royal proportions, a clear mark for the hostility of the world. But elect and reprobate are intermixed on earth, and God's eye alone infallibly distinguishes them.

St Augustine furnishes this general differentiation of the Two Cities:

> These Two Cities are made by two loves: the earthly City by love of oneself even to contempt of God; the heavenly City by love of God even to contempt of oneself. The one glories in itself, the other glories in God. The one seeks glory from men; to the other, God, witness of conscience, is its greatest glory. The one lifts up its head in its own glory: the other says to its God (Ps. iii 3), *my glory and the lifter up of my head* (*De Civitate Dei*, xiv, 28).

A Catholic, reading *The City of God*, is likely to encounter sundry things that he will disagree with. He may then apply to St Augustine what St Augustine says, writing to St Jerome: " Only to the canonical books of Scripture have I learnt to pay such awe and honour as to believe most firmly that no author of them has erred at all in his writing; but in reading other writers, however distinguished for holiness and learning, I never take a thing for true simply because it is their opinion; nor do I suppose that you would have your books read like the books of the prophets and apostles " (Letter 82). Much erudition has come to hand, and the outlook of the human mind has changed vastly, in the fifteen centuries since Augustine wrote. *The City of God* is in many respects an antiquated book. But its main line of thought is not antiquated. As a mirror of Catholic faith, as a view of the world from a Christian standpoint, it remains to this day exactly as St Augustine wrote it. St Augustine's Two Cities, Jerusalem and Babylon, reappear in St Ignatius's Two Standards. We recognise still Satan's throne of fire and smoke, and his vamping up of riches and worldly glory, culminating in huge pride; and the opposite attitude of Christ our Saviour, with his gospel of poverty and humility. Such teaching is of the essence of Christianity, and that does not change. The tone and ethos of *The City of God* is the ethos of the Church and of the true Christian to this day. In that sense *The City of God* is an immortal work.

It will now be our care to go over the salient points of the twenty-two books.

Postscriptum

Since this little outline was all written, a new stimulus has been given to the study of St Augustine by a splendid edition of the Latin text, *St Augustine's De Civitate Dei, with Introduction and Appendices*, by J. E. G. Welldon, D.D., Dean of Durham (London, S.P.C.K., 2 vols., 42s. net, 1924). It will be seen that I am in some disagreement with the Dean on the point of Sacrifice.

BOOK I

The right glorious City of God. St Augustine opens with these words. He had in mind to comfort himself for the fall of Rome the "Eternal City," with whose prosperity the very existence of human society seemed bound up. For the first time in her history, since she had attained to empire, Rome had come into the power of a foreign invader. Always a loyal citizen, Augustine was filled with grief and horror. He found comfort with St Paul: *we have not here a lasting city, but seek that which is to come* (Heb. xiii 14), and is even now, however imperfectly, on earth. He set this city, the *heavenly Jerusalem* (Gal. iv 26; Apoc. xxi 10), over against *Babylon*, pagan Rome (Apoc. xvii 5). For Rome, notwithstanding her recent Christianity, still stood for paganism. Her glories were those of a pagan city: she was saturated still with the paganism of centuries; many of her nobility remained pagan; pagan superstitions had still a great hold on her people. And pagans blamed Christianity for her fall.

Rome was not destroyed by Alaric. He plundered the city, slew many of the people, then evacuated it, leaving the buildings but little injured. The closest parallel to the catastrophe of 410 is to be found in 1529, when Rome was captured and plundered, and torrents of blood shed in her streets by the army of Charles V, under the Constable de Bourbon. De Bourbon seems to have done about as much damage as Alaric, or even more. Alaric, himself a Christian, spared the lives of all who took refuge in the churches: his soldiers even conducted people there to ensure their safety (*C. D.*, i, 1).

"And yet," writes Augustine, a patriot and a prophet;

"The Roman Empire has suffered a shock rather than a subversion, an experience that has befallen Rome at other times ere Christ's name was preached. From those previous shocks she recovered, nor in these our days are we to despair of her recovery. For who knows the will of God in this concern?" (*C. D.*, iv, 7).

Taking up the doctrine of Eccles. ix 1, 2, St Augustine observes how the good and evil things of this life are distributed pretty indiscriminately to good and evil men (i, 8). The good may sometimes deserve to share the earthly punishment of the wicked, inasmuch as through false shame and complaisance they have neglected to rebuke the evil going on around them (c. 9). Even so, what the good suffer, all turns to their good (Rom. viii 20). What though many Christian bodies went unburied? The pomp of a funeral is more for the comfort of the living than for the benefit of the dead. A good Christian can dispense with it; his resurrection to glory is secure anyhow. And yet, so far as in us lies, we should reverently consign to earth those bodies that have been the organs of the Holy Ghost (cc. 12, 13).

In cc. 16-18 St Augustine meets the taunt that God suffered Christian women to be violated by the barbarians in Alaric's train. He gives an answer, which ever since has been taken for final in the Church, that even in that hard case it would be wrong for a woman to save her honour by taking her own life. The violence is entirely the sin of the doer; the sufferer is innocent; her virginity before God is intact. "As long as the purpose of the mind holds firm, which is the sanctification also of the body, even the body does not lose its holiness by the violence of another's lust, but the steady will of continence in the mind keeps the body holy." Suicide is always sinful, and sin is not to be avoided by sin. Some martyrs, indeed, have so taken their own lives; of these Augustine writes: "I dare not pronounce any hasty judgement on these cases" (c. 26). A modern Lucretia would be warned by her confessor not to copy that pagan example: for Lucretia, see cap. 19.

The Romans distinguished *ludi scenici*, stage-plays, from *ludi circenses*, which were more like our menagerie and circus shows. The *ludi circenses* were horribly wasteful of human life in the combats of gladiators, and of men, and even women, exposed to wild beasts. Of them, however, Augustine has little to say. The advent of Christian emperors had mitigated, if not abolished, such cruelties. But the *ludi scenici* went on at Rome and in the provincial cities. Augustine in his unbridled youth witnessed them at Carthage. In *The City of God* he recurs to them again and again with horror. We have extant specimens of them in the plays of Plautus and Terence. Those plays are coarse enough; but of them St Augustine writes: "These are the more tolerable forms of stage-plays, tragedies and comedies, that is, fables of the poets for theatrical representation, involving in their composition much coarseness of theme, but anyhow free from obscenity of language, so that in the course of what are called high-class and liberal studies boys are compelled by their elders to read and study these plays" (*C. D.*, ii, 8). But, as actually staged, the plays were far worse both at Rome and Athens. They were nothing less than immodest pantomimes. "How shall I tell that man to love God, who still loves the mimic, still loves the pantomime?" asks St Augustine (*Enarr. in ps.* 36). St John Chrysostom is equally emphatic, e.g. *hom.* 28 *in* 1 *Cor.* The misery of it all was that these obscenities were exhibited in the name of religion. Stage-plays were first introduced at Rome to avert the divine anger in a pestilence (*C. D.*, i, 32; Livy, vii; Valerius Maximus, ii, 4). The Pontifex Maximus, Scipio Nasica, held in his day to be the best man in Rome, was so disgusted with them that he persuaded the Senate to stop the building of a theatre (i, 31).

Stage-plays, those spectacular obscenities, those licensed follies, were set on foot at Rome, not by the vices of men, but by the commands of your gods. It would be more tolerable for you to pay divine honours to that Scipio than to worship such gods. The gods were inferior to their Pontiff. Come, look at the facts, if your mind, so long intoxicated with error, allows you still any sober reflection. The gods, for the avoidance of a bodily pestilence, ordered stage-plays to be exhibited in their honour: the pontiff, to save a pestilence of souls, ordered the very stage to be pulled down. Choose whether of the two you will worship.

This propitiation of such deities, a propitiation most wanton, most impure, most shameless, most wicked, most filthy, the actors in which were deprived of civil rights, struck off the list of voters, recognised as base persons, declared infamous by the praiseworthy genius of Roman virtue, this propitiation, I say, of such deities, shameful, abominable, and detestable in the eyes of true religion, these lewd fables, discreditable to the gods, these shameful doings of gods, criminal and obscene, if they were really done, still more wicked and foul if they were mere inventions—this is what the whole city had to learn, and drink in with eyes and ears in public assembly; the spectators naturally assuming that what it was right for them to see represented on the stage was also right for them to copy in private life (i, 32; ii, 27).

Referring to the fact that while in Greek States actors enjoyed the full franchise, they were disfranchised at Rome, St Augustine draws up the following syllogism:

The following argument puts the whole question in a nut-shell: The Greeks put forward the major premise: *If such gods are to be worshipped, surely the actors in such plays are to be honoured.* The Romans subsume with the minor premise: *But such actors are nowise to be honoured.* The Christians draw the conclusion: *Therefore such gods are nowise to be worshipped* (ii, 13).

St Augustine adds: " They deserve not to be worshipped by virtue, who are appeased by lewdness " (i, 29).

BOOK II

St Augustine writes: "So few non-Christians have remained that, instead of their daring to reproach others for being Christians, it is rather a reproach to them that they are not Christians" (*Enarr.* 4 *in ps.* 30). The public worship of the pagan gods was forbidden by an imperial edict in A.D. 391. It remains an interesting speculation to argue how far the hearts of the multitude were really weaned from paganism. The reader will learn much from *Roman Society in the Last Century of the Western Empire*, by Samuel Dill (Macmillan). He discusses *The City of God* in pp. 59-73. He writes of it: "All that wealth of learning and subtlety of disquisition would not have been wasted by a busy and practical man in trampling out the embers of an exploded superstition" (pp. 64-65). Many Christians still remained half-pagan in sentiment. Even so in England, for a century after the Reformation, when the Government had embraced the New Learning, and by vigorous coercion endeavoured to enforce it upon the people, the hearts of a large moiety of Englishmen, for all their external compliance with the New, remained attached to the Old. The fascination of the worship of the *Dea Roma*, of the old Roman mythology, poetry, architecture, social customs and law—we know how these struck the Italian of the Renaissance; how much more potent instruments must they have been, when, within the memory of living men, they were still dominant and ruled the world! The reader of *The City of God*, then, must put up with lengthy arguments and invectives against paganism which in his eyes may look like slaying the slain.

History in its general features repeats itself. The

rupture of the *Pax Romana* by the sack of Rome in 410, and the subsequent overthrow of the Western Empire, has its analogue in our own day. The war of 1914-18 has for ever overthrown the old *Pax Europaea;* for better or for worse, Europe will never again be what she was. It was given to the Christian Church and to the Papacy gradually to build up a new Roman Peace in Christ, the glorious creation of the Middle Ages. To this St Augustine's *City of God* was a powerful aid. It was a much-read book, and guided medieval ideas. The peace of pagan Rome, like the European Peace previous to 1914, was in many respects a rotten peace. St Augustine shows powerfully what the ideal was which the disappointed pagans of his time regretted and wished to revert to. And are there not many in our own day who at heart regret, and would gladly see restored, the years of wealth, lavish expenditure, and self-indulgence, with which the nineteenth century closed and the twentieth opened? May those days be gone for ever. Here is the description of them:

> Only let it stand, they say, only let our commonwealth flourish, replete with wealth, glorious with victories, or, better still, secure in peace. What is anything else to us? Rather it is our chief concern that every man may be perpetually making money to meet his daily profuse expenditure, and to enable the stronger to lord it over the weak. . . . Let peoples applaud, not the ministers who take thought for the popular welfare, but the providers of popular amusements. Let no hard enactments be made, no impurities forbidden. Let kings take no thought of the morals, only of the tractability of their subjects. . . . Let none be brought into a criminal court except for damage done to another's property, house, or person, for annoying or hurting others; for the rest, let any man make of his own, or do with his own, or with any who will consent to his doings, simply whatever he likes. Let there be plenty of loose women on the streets for general enjoyment, for their enjoyment particularly who cannot afford to keep mistresses of their own. Let spacious mansions, lofty and elaborately

adorned, tower over the heads of passers-by; let sumptuous dinners be given according to every man's taste and means; day and night let there be gaming, drinking, vomiting, and debauchery. Let the beat of dancers' feet be heard everywhere: let theatres resound with the cries of unholy mirth, and teem with every kind of amusement, even the cruellest and the basest. Let him be accounted a public enemy, who has no mind for this style of happiness. Whoever attempts its alteration or removal, let the democracy refuse him a hearing, turn him out of house and home; banish him from the number of the living. Let them be accounted true gods, who have procured for peoples this prosperity, and guarded it when gained. Let them be worshipped as they will, let them call for the games that they choose: all that we expect of them is that this our prosperity may have nothing to fear from war, from pestilence, from any calamity (*C. D.*, ii, 20).

This sort of temporal prosperity the pagans looked to their gods to provide, not morality and virtue. Pagan worship did not make for morality and virtue, quite the reverse. Augustine instances what he had himself often witnessed, of the worship of the goddess called by Africans *Coelestis*, "the heavenly," apparently Venus. The more reputable defenders of these rites maintained that they were symbolical of high and holy truths, a symbolism which was taught to a select few in the temples. Augustine replies: "What is creditable is hidden away, what is discreditable is open to the gaze of all (*decus latet et dedecus patet*). The evil that is enacted gathers all spectators; whatever good is said finds hardly any hearers. Thus the virtuous few are caught without the profligate majority being corrected. When and where the votaries of Coelestis heard precepts of chastity, we know not: all I know is that, right in front of the shrine where we saw that idol set up, were gathered crowds from all sides, scarce finding standing-room, who gazed with all their eyes at the plays that were being acted: all functions of obscenity were exhibited" (ii, 4, 26). All this, be it remembered, in the name of religion! There is some truth in the famous line of Lucretius:

Tantum relligio potuit suadere malorum.

Augustine contrasts the sobriety and purity of the Christian worship, and appeals to the Romans of his day:

> These rather be thy desires, thou glorious Roman genius, descendant of the Reguli, the Scaevolas, the Scipios, the Fabricii; these rather be thy desires; see the difference between these Christian rites and those hideous, empty, and most fallacious antics of evil spirits. Whatever praiseworthy natural qualities distinguish thee, it is only by true piety that they can be purified and made perfect; by impiety they are ruined and laid open to punishment (ii, 29).

The above (*si quid in te laudabile naturaliter eminet*) is a noteworthy acknowledgement from St Augustine that there are such things as natural virtues, which the Jansenists, claiming his support, denied.

BOOK III

In this book St Augustine ransacks Roman annals to show, what there is no difficulty in evincing, that temporal calamities—and it was against these alone that the aid of pagan deities was invoked—did not begin with Christianity, but were frequent from the earliest times. He observes that the civil war between Marius and Sulla, nearly a century before Christ, made greater havoc at Rome than Attila's raid. "The Goths," he says, "spared the lives of so many senators, that the wonder is that they killed any at all" (c. 29). He quotes Livy, book xc, for a plague of locusts which befell Africa about the same time:

> After the locusts had wasted the trees, fruit and leaf, they say that a huge, countless crowd of them fell into the sea; whereupon from the vitiation of the air by their dead bodies, flung upon the beach, such a pestilence arose that 800,000 persons perished in Massinissa's kingdom (Algiers) alone, and many more in the lands nearest the shore. . . . What of this would not pagan folly attribute to the Christian religion, if they saw it happening in Christian times? And yet they do not attribute such things to their gods (c. 31).

The following is a neat summary of a momentous period of Roman history:

> Next comes the war of Pompey and Caesar. Pompey had been a follower of Sulla, and had attained to the level of his power, or even risen above it. Caesar could not endure Pompey's power, simply because he had it not himself. He overcame and slew him, and went beyond him in power. The Romans next came under another Caesar, afterwards called Augustus, in whose reign Christ was born. Augustus waged many civil wars with many adversaries. In these wars many illustrious men perished, and among them the eloquent political theorist, Cicero. Caius (Julius)

Caesar, victorious over Pompey, had used his civil victory with clemency, and granted his opponents their lives and honours. But seeing him aiming at kingly power, a conspiracy of senatorial nobles murdered him in the very senate-house in the name of republican liberty. A man very unequal to Caesar in character, one stained and debauched with all vices, was in the way of rivalling Caesar's power. This was Mark Antony, against whom Cicero stood out, offering a vigorous resistance in the name of his country's liberty. By this time there had risen into prominence another Caesar, son by adoption of the former Caius Caesar, a youth of wonderful ability, who, as I said, was afterwards called Augustus. Cicero favoured this youthful Caesar to gain his support against Antony. He hoped that he would overthrow and crush Antony's domination, and restore liberty to the republic. Blind man, destitute of foresight of the future! That very youth, whose dignity and power he was fostering, was to hand over Cicero to Antony unto death as a pledge of their concord, and subject to his own sway that liberty of the republic so loudly voiced by the rator (*G. D.*, iii, 30).

BOOK IV

In two interesting chapters (cc. 3, 15), St Augustine argues that Empire is not an unmixed blessing. If the imperial power is wielded by good men, it is a blessing indeed, but rather to subjects than to rulers. If bad men rule, their rule is a curse to themselves; but spiritually, they cannot hurt the good, unless the good wilfully fall away. *Non nocet nisi iniquitas propria*, a favourite saying of St John Chrysostom.

The curious thing in this book is the enumeration of Roman deities, a deity to preside over every function of life. To this curious fact St Augustine frequently returns (see *C. D.*, iv, 8, 11, 21; vi, 9; vii, 3; xix, 17). Thus Vaticanus presided over the wailings (*vagitus*) of children, Cunina over their cradles (*cunae*), Collatina over hills (*colles*), Valorica over valleys; Seia, Segetia, Tutilina, Nodotus, and six others were concerned with the crops; Forculus looked after the door (*fores*), Cardea cared for the hinges (*cardines*), Limentinus for the threshold (*limen*); while to Cloacina was committed the important matter of the drainage (*cloaca*). "How can one gather in one book," asks Augustine, "the names of all the gods, or goddesses, which pagan authors have scarce been able to comprise in volumes, assigning proper offices of deity to every possible concern?" Some said that all these deities represented nothing but various offices of the one Jupiter; some made Jupiter the soul of the world (iv, 11, 12; vii, 11). St Augustine quotes from Varro's *Antiquities*—and further it is affirmed in Plutarch's *Life of Numa*, ch. viii, *cf.* Pliny, *Historia Naturalis*, xxxiv, 4—that the Romans for 170 years had no idols, or images of gods, in their worship. Varro remarks: "Had that custom stood, religion would be purer than it is at present." Did this early absence of images point to monotheism, or to fetish-worship, or perhaps star-worship ?

BOOK V

WAS the growth of the Roman Empire brought about by the stars? Did the stars rule it, or did they simply indicate the doom of fate? And what is fate? "If by *fate* anyone means the will or power of God, let him keep his meaning, but mend his language: for *fate* commonly means a necessary process which will have its way apart from the will of God and of men" (cc. 1, 8). The vanity of horoscopes is proved by the different life-histories of twins, born together under the same star. Jacob and Esau are instanced, and Augustine adds an experience of his own.

> We know a pair of twins, both still alive and flourishing, as like one another in bodily appearance as persons of different sex can possibly be; but in avocation and walk of life so different that the brother is in the suite of the governor of the province, and is nearly always away from home, the sister never leaves her home in the country; the brother is married, and is the father of a large family, the sister is a maiden consecrate to God (cc. 2, 4-6).

St Augustine now gets upon a favourite theme, God's foreknowledge of what man will do, man's will still remaining free in doing it. He observes that Cicero (*De divinatione*, ii) did not see his way to holding both these positions together, and, rather than deny human free will, denied divine foreknowledge. Unreasonably, says Augustine, because God sees events in the causes that bring them about, among which causes human wills figure; viewing the human will, then, God sees what that will will elect to do. Such seems to be the meaning of St Augustine's argument:

> It does not follow that, if the order of all causes is known to God for certain, therefore there is nothing left in the

power of our free will. Our very wills are in the order of causes, which order is known for certain to God, and is contained in his foreknowledge; for human wills are causes of human works. And, therefore, he who has foreknown the causes of all things, cannot possibly have been ignorant of our wills among those causes, which wills he has foreknown as causes of our works (*C. D.*, v, 9).

The argument is open to the reply, that free acts, as such, are not antecedently and determinately contained in the will that elicits them; therefore no antecedent knowledge of the will can be any sure knowledge of the act to come of it. The usual answer now given is clearer, falling back upon the eternity of God. To God (*C. D.*, xi, 21) the future is as the present; there is no more difficulty in the Eternal foreseeing what we will do than in the Omniscient seeing what we are doing, and doing freely.

Twelve years later, in his *De correptione et gratia*, St Augustine worked this topic out with greater explicitness; here he does not refer to grace at all. Nor, though he comes near it, does he raise the question, started by Molina, as to whether God knows what a man freely would do, if he were placed in circumstances in which he never will be placed. Augustine left many things unsettled for seventeenth-century theologians to dispute about.

St Augustine argues the dependence of all corporeal nature upon the guidance of spirit in its every action, a thesis to debate in the philosophical schools.

In God's will is vested the sovereign power, which aids the good wills of created spirits, judges evil wills, orders all wills; gives powers to some, and denies them to others. As God is the Creator of all natures, so he is the giver of all powers, but not of all volitions. Evil volitions are not of him, because they are against that nature which is of him. Bodily things are subject to wills, some to our wills, that is, to the wills of all mortal animals, and of men more than of beasts. Some are subject to the wills of angels, but all are chiefly subject to the will of God. To that will all wills are subject, because they have no power beyond that which he grants them. The one cause that is active, and not passive (*quae facit, nec fit*) is God. Other causes are both active and passive, as are all created spirits, especially rational spirits. But bodily causes, being passive rather than active, are not to be counted among efficient causes, because their power is limited to that which the wills of spirits make of them (*hoc possunt quod ex ipsis faciunt spirituum voluntates*).

St Augustine, as is well known, saw no hope of any sort of happiness awaiting pagans in the life to come. And in this view many have concurred. I should not be so ready to pronounce sentence on so large a portion of mankind, God's creatures, after all, human beings for whom Christ died. If we are unable to formulate any definite scheme of hope for them, then we had better fall back upon our ignorance, avowing with Newman that "we do not understand the dispensation of paganism" (*University Sermons*, pp. 21, 23). And has not the Supreme Judge himself warned us not to forestall his sentence? *Judge not* (Matt. vii 1). Thus, then, St Augustine writes of the ancient Romans:

God was not minded to give them life everlasting with his holy angels in his heavenly City. True piety leads to that society, and true piety pays the worship, called by the Greeks *latria*, to the one true God alone. If, then, God did not grant them this earthly glory of a surpassing empire, there would be no reward rendered to their good conduct. —that is, to the virtues whereby they strove to arrive at this great glory. Of people of this stamp, who seem to do some good in order to reap glory from men, the Lord also says: *Amen, I say unto you, they have received their reward* (Matt. vi 2). So then these Romans made light of their private interests for the sake of the common weal, or republic, and for the augmentation of its treasure; they withstood avarice, they generously consulted their country's good, they committed no offence against their own laws, they indulged in no unlawful gratification; they held on in such practices as being the true way to honour, empire, glory; so it has come to be that they have been honoured nearly all the world over; they have imposed the laws of their empire upon many nations; they have at this day a glorious name in literature and history among almost all mankind. They have no reason to complain of the justice of the supreme and true God: *they have received their reward.* Quite other is the reward of the Saints, who here suffer obloquy for the City of God, a thing odious to the lovers of this world. That City is everlasting: no births there, because no deaths (*ibi nullus oritur, quia nullus moritur*). There is true and full happiness, not a goddess (*cf.* iv 23), but a gift of God. Thence we have received the pledge of faith for so long as on pilgrimage we aspire to the beauty of that City. There the sun does not rise upon good and bad (Matt. v 45), but the Sun of Justice protects the good alone. There will be no great industry to enrich the public treasury at the expense of private poverty; there will be a common treasure of truth. Thus it was not only that worldly reward might be rendered to worldly men that the Roman Empire was raised to such a height of human glory, but also that the citizens of that everlasting City, during their pilgrimage here, may diligently and soberly consider those examples, and reflect how much love is due to their heavenly country in view of life everlasting, if an earthly city was so much loved by Roman citizens in view of human glory (v, cc. 15, 16; *cf.* c. 18 for amplification of the last sentence).

African Augustine speaks with exultation of the Emperor Caracalla's extension of the Roman citizenship to all subjects of the empire—" a most gracious and humane act " (*gratissime atque humanissime factum*), " making that the right of all, which was before the privilege of a few " (c. 17), well illustrated by Acts xxii 25-29. In consequence, the title of Senator became a sort of knighthood, a mere title of honour. " Are there not many Senators in other lands who do not know Rome even by sight ?" (c. 17).

St Augustine, however, modestly disclaims having penetrated the divine counsels in the rise of the Roman power. " There may be some cause more deeply hidden, rather known to God than us " (c. 19). He goes on: " But all truly pious men must avow that, without true piety, that is, without the worship of the true God, no man can have true virtue." This he repeats even more emphatically (xix, 25). It may be remarked that as God may be known by reason, apart from revelation, the worship of the true God is philosophically possible away from the revelation and grace of Christ. Nor are we able to set limits to the grace of Christ. It may stream through invisible channels where the Gospel is not preached (*cf.* the propositions of Quesnel condemned in the *Unigenitus*, Nos. 26-29). St Augustine's eyes beheld so much of the revolting rites of paganism, that his mind hardly adverted sufficiently to the likelihood, now confirmed by enquiry and the comparative study of religions, of some glimmer of monotheism shining at the back of polytheistic theologies (*cf.* iv, 31).

St Augustine (v, 23) gives a valuable piece of contemporary history, the defeat and slaughter of Rhadagaisus, King of the Goths, by Stilicho, the general of the Emperor Honorius, A.D. 406. "The story we heard at Carthage," he says, "was, that the pagans in Rhadagaisus's army believed and boasted everywhere that they were invincible under the protection of their gods, to whom their king offered daily sacrifice, while the cessation and prohibition of such sacrifices cut off the Romans from all hope of victory." Augustine writes triumphantly, *nutu summae majestatis oppressus est.*

The happiness of a Christian Emperor, he says, lies not in length of reign or victories, which God sometimes grants to the heathen, but in being just, proof against flattery, placable, chaste—and that not for ostentation, but for heaven. He recites the praises of Constantine and Theodosius, a golden foil to pagan glories (cc. 24-26).

BOOK VI

HAVING shown that the gods of paganism are powerless to guarantee their worshippers happiness in this world, Augustine goes on to enquire whether they can afford men happiness after death. It is plain that their votaries generally set no store by such ultramundane beatitude, and never expected their gods to bestow it upon them. The enquiry brings Augustine across the more spiritually-minded pagans, their religious historians and philosophers. And first he is confronted with the figure of Marcus Terentius Varro, Varro whom Cicero, his contemporary and friend, calls " the best critic and most learned man in Rome " (vi, 2), and whom he compliments upon his forty-one books of *Antiquities* in these terms: " We were to seek in our own city, losing our way like strangers: your books have brought us home, so that now we can recognise who and where we are. You have made clear the age of our city, its chronology, its religious canons, its priestly traditions, its topography, its military discipline, the names, characters, offices, causes of all things in it, divine and human " (Cicero, *Quaest. Academ.*, i, 3, quoted in *C. D.*, vi, 2). St Augustine says of Varro (*ibid.*): " He read so much that we wonder he had time to write anything; he wrote as much as we can scarcely believe any one man ever managed to read "—a saying not inapplicable to Augustine himself. Augustine was a bishop, and Varro at one time governed a province. Varro's *Antiquities* is a treasure the loss of which we deplore; Augustine made great use of it, and gives a summary of its contents (vi, 3), twenty-five books on things human, sixteen on things divine. Varro followed the Chief Pontiff Scaevola, of whom St Augustine writes (*C. D.*, iv, 27):

Scaevola argued three traditional kinds of gods, one by the tradition of poets, a second by the tradition of philosophers, the third by the tradition of statesmen. The first tradition he says is nugatory, as containing many fictions unworthy of gods; the second is ill-suited for States, as containing avowals hurtful for the people to know, for instance, that Hercules, Aesculapius, Castor, and Pollux were men, and died the deaths of men; and that of gods who really were gods the cities have not true images, that a true god has neither sex, nor age, nor bodily lineaments. These things the Pontiff does not wish the people to know, not that he thinks them false. He considers it, therefore, expedient for States to be deceived in the matter of religion. And Varro, in his books on things divine, does not hesitate to say the same.

These are Varro's own words, quoted by Augustine, *C. D.*, vi, 5:

They call that theology *mythical*, which poets use; *natural*, which is followed by philosophers; *civil*, which is taken up by States. As for the first, it contains many fictions unworthy of the dignity and nature of immortal beings, as that one deity [Minerva] was born from the head of another [Jupiter], another [Vulcan] from his [Jupiter's] thigh, a third [Saturn] from the drops of another's [Uranus's] blood; that gods have committed theft and adultery, and been [Apollo] in the service of man; in fine, all those deeds are attributed to gods which cannot be related, I do not say of man, but even of the vilest of mankind. The second kind of theology, which I have mentioned, is that which philosophers have bequeathed to us in many books, enquiring who the gods are, where they are, what is their race and nature; whether they are from a given time or have been from eternity; whether they are made of fire, as Heraclitus believes, or of numbers, as Pythagoras holds, or of atoms, as says Epicurus; and other like opinions, more tolerable to listen to within the walls of a lecture-room than out in the open air in the market-place. The third theology is what citizens, priests especially, ought to know and administer, teaching what gods it is fitting to worship in public, and with what rites and sacrifices. The first theology is most suited for the theatre, the second for the world of thought (*ad mundum*), the third for public life (*ad urbem*).

"Who does not see," cries St Augustine, "to which he has assigned the palm? Clearly to the second, which he has called the theology of philosophers." He proceeds to apostrophise Varro:

O Marcus Varro, most acute of critics, and beyond doubt most learned of men, but still *a man, not God* (Ezech. xxviii 2), nor raised up by the Spirit of God to such height of truth and liberty as to see and tell forth the things of God, thou seest how Divinity ought to stand clear of human triflings and lies; but thou art afraid to offend the vicious opinions and customs of peoples, enacted in the popular superstitions! What avails here thy genius, most excellent, but human? What does thy erudition, still human, though manifold and enormous, do to rescue thee in this pass? Thou desirest to worship the gods that are by nature, thou art forced to recognise those that are established by the State (*naturales deos colere cupis, civiles cogeris*, vi, 6).

We are indebted to Augustine for these quotations from a great work otherwise lost to us. Let us then listen to Varro again (*apud C. D.*, vii, 17):

I ought not to be found fault with for setting down in this treatise doubtful opinions about the gods. Whoever thinks that a decided view is necessary and obtainable, let him decide for himself, when he has heard what I have to say. . . . To quote Xenophanes of Colophon, "I shall put down my conjectures, not my convictions. It is man's to have opinions on these questions, it is God's to have knowledge" (*hominis est haec opinari, Dei scire*).

This is the state of mind that Christian revelation had to meet, and still has to meet. Varro's private opinions in theology are given in detail thus:

Varro says, treating of natural theology, that he considers God to be the soul of the universe, and that this universe itself is God; but that as a wise man, though made up of body and soul, is called *wise* from his soul, so the universe is called *God* from its mind, though made up of mind and body. Here he seems in some sort to confess one God; but, wishing to leave room also for many gods, he adds that "the universe is divided into two parts, heaven and earth;

and heaven again into two parts, the upper and lower air; and earth again into water and dry land; that of these four elements the upper air is highest, the lower air next, water third, dry land lowest; that all these four elements are full of souls, immortal souls in the upper and lower air, mortal in water and on dry land; that from the highest sphere of heaven to the sphere of the moon [see the Ptolemaic astronomy, which lasted till Copernicus] the ethereal souls are the constellations and stars, and that these heavenly gods are beheld, not with the mind's eye alone, but with the eye of the body [assisted by telescope and spectroscope and photographic plate], but that within the sphere of the moon and the high watersheds (*cacumina*) of clouds and winds are other souls, beheld with the mind's eye, but not with bodily eyes, and these are called heroes, and household gods and fairies (*genios*). And this was not Varro's view alone, but of many philosophers.

How has the march of science shattered this theology, leaving untouched St Augustine's faith!

Leaving the natural theology of the philosophers alone for the present, St Augustine goes on to ask how life everlasting can possibly be sought at the hands of the deities of either the mythical or the civil theology—*i.e.*, the gods either of poets or of popular religion (vi, 6). The latter are worse than the former; the secret rites of the temple are more obscene than the open immodesties of the stage.

We should rather be grateful to the gentlemen of the stage, who have spared the eyes of men, and not made an open spectacle of all that is concealed within the walls of sacred edifices. What good opinion can we form of that portion of their rites which is shrouded in darkness, when what does come to light is so detestable? What they do in secret by the agency of these victims of self-mutilation, they must know for themselves. Let them persuade whom they can, that they teach some lesson of holiness by the agency of such creatures. We do not know what they do, but we know who their agents are. We know what is acted on the stage, where never eunuch or effeminate person has been suffered to tread the boards. [St John Chrysostom may be alleged to the contrary]: yet on the stage they do things shocking and unseemly. What, then, are those sacred rites, for which in the name of holiness there are chosen such performers as even the obscenity of the theatre refuses to employ? (*C. D.*, vi, 7).

Augustine must have bethought him of St Paul's words: *The things done by them in secret it is shameful even to utter* (Eph. v 12). Seneca in a work now lost, but quoted here (*C. D.*, vi, 11), and by Tertullian, *Apol.* 12, goes beyond Varro in condemning the "Civil," or State religion. "All this crowd of ignoble deities," he writes, "which a lengthy superstition has huddled together in length of years, we shall so adore as to remember that the worship of them is rather a convention than a reality (*magis ad morem quam ad rem pertinere*)." Thus, Augustine remarks, Seneca in his character of illustrious senator of the Roman people, "adored what he blamed" (*quod culpabat adorabat*). "How then," Augustine concludes once more, "shall the power of giving life everlasting be attributed to any of these gods!" (*C. D.*, vi, 8).

BOOK VII

The argument makes little advance in this Book. St Augustine, in the Preface to it, avers that for " nimbler and better-gifted minds, the reasoning of the previous Books is enough and more than enough." Certainly it is enough for us, who have never felt the glamour of Roman polytheism as a present fascination before our eyes. Our interest in this Book is one of curiosity for the erudition which it supplies.

First we learn (c. 1) that *deitas*, so familiar a word in modern Latin, was a new coinage in St Augustine's time, the older word being *divinitas*. We are given a list from Varro of *dii selecti*, twelve male and eight female, whose morals, Augustine observes, were even worse than those of the more ignoble residue of the court of polytheism (cc. 2-4). There was a tendency to make the minor deities (see Book IV), not distinct individuals, but Jupiter himself, or some Nature Power, or World-Soul, working in so many various natural operations (cc. 9-16, 19-24). After more examples of the unnatural turpitudes by which such gods were considered to be honoured, St Augustine goes on:

Is it to " select gods " such as these that man is to be consecrated, to the end that he may attain happiness after death, when for such consecration he cannot live virtuously before death, subject to such foul superstitions, and bound over to unclean demons? But all this, I am told, is to be referred to Nature-worship. See rather whether it be not to the worship of the Unnatural (*Sed haec omnia referuntur ad mundum. Vide ne potius ad immundum*). But we look rather for a soul that, borne up by true religion, shall not adore the world for her god, but take the world for the work of God, and praise it accordingly; and, so cleansed from the filth of the world, shall arrive clean and pure to God, who created the world (c. 26).

Augustine tells a curious story from Varro about Numa, the second King of Rome, and institutor of Roman religion. These are Varro's words, quoted in *C. D.*, vii, 34; Plutarch has the story in his *Life of Numa*, c. 22.

There was a certain Terentius, who had a farm near the Janiculum. A ploughman in his employment, passing his plough near the tomb of Numa Pompilius, turned up from the earth his books, containing an account of the reasons for the religious rites that he had set on foot. Terentius took the manuscript to the City Praetor. The Praetor, after reading the first pages, thought the document so important that he laid it before the Senate. The leading men of the City read some of the reasons assigned for this and that institution; whereupon, animated by religious motives, as befitted Conscript Fathers, the Senate voted that the Praetor do burn those books.

Augustine surmises that the origins of Roman religion, here revealed, were so discreditable that Numa buried the record, and the Senate, "in agreement with the dead Numa," burnt it. Numa was supposed to have gained his mystic lore by hydromancy, or gazing at surfaces of water, perhaps a first essay towards crystal-gazing.

St Augustine winds up with this eloquent counter-plea for Christian worship:

We worship that God who has appointed for the natures that he has created the beginnings and ends of their existence and activities, who holds in his hand, knows and disposes of, the causes of all things; who has organised the potentiality of seeds; who has infused a rational soul into such living creatures as he would; who has given also the faculty and use of speech; who has assigned the function of foretelling the future to such spirits as he pleased, and through whom he pleases himself foretells the future, and through whom he pleases repels attacks of illness; who, when mankind have to be amended and chastised by war, regulates the commencements, developments, and issues of wars; who has created and governs and tempers to the needs of the immense kingdom of nature the vehement and violent element of fire in this world;[1] who is creator and ruler of all waters; who has made the sun brightest of corporal lights, and given it its proper power and motion; who does not withdraw due dominion and power even from hell; who puts in their place and assigns to competent natures, whether on land or water, the seeds and aliments of mortal beings; who establishes and fertilises the earth; who grants its fruits to animals and men; who knows and ordains causes, not only principal but secondary also; who has appointed for the moon its orbit; who affords scope in sky and earth for changes of place; who has bestowed on human minds that he has created the knowledge of various arts for the aid of life and nature; who has instituted the union of male and female in aid of the propagation of offspring; who has granted the gift of earthly fire for the comfort of gatherings of men, that they might use it for warmth and light. All these are the makings and the doings of the one true God, but as God, that is, of one who is whole and entire everywhere, shut up in no places, bound by no ties, divided into no parts, in no way changeable, filling heaven and earth with his present power, while his nature has no need of them. And while administering all things that he has created, he allows them to exercise and carry into act their own proper activities.[2]

These several functions of the one true God, we must remember, were assigned by paganism to so many separate deities, a fact which determines this enumeration.

[1] " They all are fire, and every one doth burn," says Shakespeare's Julius Caesar of the (fixed) stars.

[2] And therefore, we may argue (v, c. 9), even material things are not destitute of their own proper active forces.

BOOK VIII

The main invective against the pagan polytheism of Rome is now complete. St Augustine passes from pagan theology to pagan philosophy, and argues that the latter is as incompetent as the former to guide men to everlasting happiness. In other words, Augustine has said all he had to say on *mythical* and *civil* theology—*i.e.*, the polytheism of the stage and of the temple; his concern in these Books VIII, IX, X, is *natural* theology, as Varro terms it—*i.e.*, the speculations of heathen philosophy on things divine.

The glory of Plato as a philosopher, says Augustine, throws all other philosophers into the shade (viii, 4). He writes, indeed, of Aristotle that " he was a man of excellent genius, and, though inferior in eloquence to Plato, yet easily ahead of many " (viii, 12). But Aristotle's star did not shine in the West till the Arabian philosophers took him up, and after them St Thomas. Augustine and the Christian Fathers were Platonists for a thousand years. This is to be ascribed, not so much to the study of Plato's actual writings, as to the dominance of Neo-Platonism, the Oriental, mystical Platonism of Plotinus, Jamblichus, Porphyry, and (in Africa) Apuleius (viii, 12). It does not appear that St Augustine read Plato in the original. Greek was disliked in Roman Africa, a dislike of old standing, from the days when Greek, Etruscan, and Carthaginian were rivals for the commerce of the Mediterranean. There was more Latin and less Greek spoken at Carthage than at Rome. The liturgy of the early Church was in Latin in Africa, while it was still in Greek at Rome. Augustine drank in his Platonism through Latin channels.

The division of philosophy into "moral," "natural," and "rational," or, as we should say, into moral science, physics (including metaphysics), and logic, which St Augustine attributes to Plato (viii, 4), is not found in Plato's own writings; it was the work of the Platonists who followed him. In all these three branches St Augustine evinces Plato's superiority and nearer approach to Christian truth (cc. 6, 7, 8). Plato grasped the truth of the spirituality of God; and though he did not know him as Creator out of nothing, he understood that the whole order and bearing of the universe was of God; he insisted on the transcendent excellence of things intellectual above things corporeal; he placed the final happiness of man in the contemplation of an incorporeal truth and goodness, by which—as Augustine supposes, and supposes with a fair measure of likelihood—Plato must have meant God. But on this identification of the Ideal Good and the Ideal Beauty with God, the Neo-Platonists were more explicit than Plato. Augustine writes:

> He (Plato) says that the true and sovereign good is God; hence he makes the philosopher to be "a lover of God," so that, since philosophy tends to happiness as its goal, he who loves God is happy in the enjoyment of God (viii, 8).

To be exact, we must observe that Plato's phrase for the sovereign good is not "God," but "the Idea of Good," or "ideal Goodness" (*Republic*, vi, 508 E); also that he does not call the philosopher *amator Dei*, "a lover of God," but θεοφιλής "loved by God" (*Republic*, 612 E *seq.*), as also does Aristotle (*Ethics*, x, c. 8).

Augustine's Platonism was Neo-Platonism. Neo-Platonism differed from Plato's original in the development of "angel-worship." *Angel*, meaning "messenger," is a Biblical word, not used by the Platonists. Their word was δαίμων, or δαιμόνιον, in St Augustine *daemon*, the English *demon*, which, however, we use only of a *bad angel*. Angels are either good or bad; but all *demons* to our ears are bad; *daemones* may be either one or the other. In this, the Neo-Platonists came under Oriental influences, particularly Babylonian and Persian. Central Asia was the native home of angel-worship and demonology. These influences affected the later Judaism, also early Christianity. Witness St Paul's Epistle to the Colossians, a treatise insisting on the subordination of angels to the Word Incarnate (see especially i 16; ii 15, 18; and Heb. i 5-14).

There are two chief passages in Plato dealing with *daemones*. The one is in the *Symposion*, 203 A: "God has no intercourse with man: it is through the world of angels (τοῦ δαιμονίου, 202 E), which intervenes between God and mortality, that all the dealing and conversation that passes between gods and men is carried on." So, too, said Apuleius and the Neo-Platonists (*C. D.*, viii, 14).

The other passage is from the *Timaeus*, 40 D-41 D, ch. xiii, too long and too fanciful for quotation, but it comes to this: The Supreme God fashioned and formed a host of inferior gods, who were the deities of Greek mythology, including the stars. To these inferior deities he committed the making of human souls, who were to be distributed among the stars till it was time for them to be embodied as men. The whole conception is wildly absurd; but this absurd, or, if you will, romantic and mystic, element in Plato made the favourite pabulum of Neo-Platonism. Archer-Hind, in his Introduction to the *Timaeus*, well observes: "Not one of Plato's writings exercised so powerful an influence on subsequent Greek thought; not one was the object of such earnest study, such constant reference. Cicero was moved to translate it into Latin; Apuleius gives for an account of the Platonic philosophy little else but a partial abstract of the *Timaeus*, with some ethical supplement from the *Republic*. . . . As for the Neo-Platonic school, how completely their thought was dominated by the *Timaeus*, despite the incongruous and almost monstrous accretions which some of them superimposed, is manifest to any reader of Plotinos or Proklos."

St Augustine, then, having expressed his high admiration of Plato, and his wonder whether the travelled Athenian had not somewhere heard something of the contents of the Hebrew Scriptures, particularly of that great Word, so germane to his own philosophy, *I am who am*[1] (Exod. iii 14; see *C. D.*, viii, 11), for the rest leaves Plato, and deals with the *daemones* of the Neo-Platonists. It must be confessed that under the head of *daemones*, or along with them, the Neo-Platonists contrived to introduce the gods of the old mythology. Even Plato, like his master Socrates, had been willing to accept their worship, purged only of the disedifying stories so constantly vituperated by Augustine (*cf. Republic*, iii). He was also willing to admit among *daemones* the spirits of good and brave men departed (*Republic*, v, 468-9). It is no surprise, then, to find the Platonists (and Varro, *C. D.*, vii, 6, above quoted) peopling the universe with gods in heaven, men on earth, *daemones* in mid-air (*C. D.*, viii, 14). Thus Neo-Platonism was prone to relapse into polytheism, and to revive, in reference to the *daemones* the lewd stories and lewd scenic representations of that cult, for these *daemones* were supposed to have bodies, and with bodies the passions of men (viii, cc. 16-18).

St Augustine's authority in this part of his work is the African Latin writer Apuleius, born at Madaura in A.D. 125, priest of the Emperor at Carthage, where statues erected to his honour stood in St Augustine's time. His chief work, *The Golden Ass*, has come down to us. He also wrote on the *Genius* (*daemon*) *of Socrates*, and on *Plato and his Doctrines*, which latter work furnished Augustine with most of his knowledge of Plato. Apuleius has been called "the evening star of Platonism, and morning-star of Neo-Platonism." He was devoted to *daemones*, and was accused of practising magic through them (c. 19). He ascribed to

[1] In the Greek, ἐγώ εἰμι ὁ ὤν: compare the Platonic αὐτὸ τὸ ὄν. The phrase in Exodus is personal and living, the Platonic phrase not formally such.

them (c. 18) the office of messengers, which Christianity ascribes to angels; only, in his representation, they were sadly lacking in the purity of angels. Apuleius thought them worthy of divine honours (c. 17); Augustine held them in horror. In fact, he recognised in them those fallen angels whom we call devils.

> It is in no way credible, what Apuleius and philosophers of his school try to persuade us, that *daemones* are intermediaries and interpreters between gods and men, bearing hence our petitions and thence the succour of the gods. Rather we must understand them to be spirits obstinately bent on doing hurt, utterly alien from righteousness, swollen with pride, livid with envy, cunning to deceive, dwelling in this mid-air, because they are cast down from the height of the higher heaven (c. 22).

He goes on to say that these demons have persuaded many that they are gods; others, that they are messengers and intermediaries of gods; while Apuleius, and after him the Neo-Platonists, seeing well that these demons are not gods, for the evil they do (*cf.* Plato, *Republic*, ii, 379), still "dare not declare them unworthy of divine honour, for fear of offending the multitudes, by whom they see them served with inveterate superstition in so many rites and temples" (*ibid.*, c. 22).

The Egyptians had a deity called Thoth, whom the Greeks identified with Hermes (Mercury). Many spurious writings were put forward in his name, chiefly the *Poimander*, ascribed to Hermes Trismegistus (thrice-great), and still extant. The works that go under the name of Hermes were really written in the Christian era, and contain obvious allusions to Christianity. St Augustine accepted them as the prophecies of a prophet who knew the one true God, Creator of the world, and yet would have men go on worshipping idols, and who lamented the time, evidently that of the Christian emperors, when idols would be destroyed, and Egypt be covered with shrines of Christian martyrs. Referring to the passage of the *Timaeus*, 40-41, already cited, this pseudo-Hermes says that as the Eternal God has made other eternal deities in his own likeness, so man makes temporary deities, statues of himself, and induces spirits to come and live in them, and thereby endow them with prophetic and healing powers. Such was the account of idols rendered by this evidently Platonist writer (*C.D.*, viii, 23-26). This leads St Augustine to give the following valuable testimony to the honour paid to the martyrs in his day:

We do not set up temples, priesthoods, and sacrifices for our martyrs, because they are not our gods, but their God is our God. We do certainly honour their shrines[1] as shrines of holy men of God, who have fought for the truth even to bodily death, that true religion might be known and false and fictitious religions confuted. But who ever heard of any priest of the faithful, standing at an altar set up over the holy body of a martyr to the honour and worship of God, and saying in the prayers: "I offer thee sacrifice, Peter, or Paul, or Cyprian?"[2] since what is offered at their shrines is offered to God, who made them both men and martyrs, that by such celebration we may return thanks to God for their victories, and call God to aid, that by the renewal of their memory we may be incited to imitation of such crowns and palms of martyrdom. All marks of homage of pious persons, then, that are paid in places sacred to martyrs are adornments of shrines, not rites or sacrifices offered to the dead as gods. Even they who bring thither their offerings of food—which is not the practice of the better sort of Christians, and in most countries there is no such custom[3]—lay them there, pray, and take them away either to eat themselves or give therewith to the poor, wishing them to be sanctified through the merits of the martyrs in the name of the God of martyrs. He well knows that these are not sacrifices to the martyrs, who knows the one sacrifice of Christians that is offered there (viii, 27).[4]

[1] *Memorias.* This use of *memoria*, μνημεῖον, is abundantly illustrated in xxii, 8.

[2] Quoted in the Council of Trent, Sess. 22, cap. 3.

[3] St Augustine's own mother, Monica, had followed this practice in Africa; at Milan she found it prohibited by St Ambrose (*Confess.*, vi, 2).

[4] The Mass that was offered over the relics of martyrs in Augustine's day as in our own. No priest would dream of offering in sacrifice to Peter the Body and Blood of Peter's Lord (*cf.* x, 20).

BOOK IX

THE materials of this Book are very slightly strung together, arguing the work of a much-occupied bishop, who had to snatch moments of rare leisure for his *City of God*, and apparently died before he could find time for a thorough revision. Two only corrections, and those quite insignificant, are made in *Retractationes*, ii, 43.

The argument of the book is contained in c. 2:

> This Book ought to contain a discussion of any distinction that Platonists may wish to draw, not between gods among themselves, seeing that they say that gods are all good; nor, again, of any distinction between gods and angels (*daemones*), seeing that they remove the gods by a wide interval from men, and place the angels midway between gods and men: the distinction of various sorts of angels is the question at present before us. It is the habit of most philosophers to speak of some angels as good, others as bad. Be this the opinion of Platonists or of any others, the discussion of it must nowise be neglected. There is danger of an enquirer, thinking to follow good angels, who shall be his mediators with the gods, taking all angels to be good, and endeavouring through them to find favour with the gods and be with them after death, and so being ensnared and deceived by the craft of malignant spirits, and wandering far from the true God, with whom alone, and in whom alone, and of whom alone the rational and intellectual human soul can be happy.

And as to the reader it might readily recur that Christian theology also points to good angels, whose intercession avails to lead us to God, St Augustine's reply is that the *daemones*, who figure in the pages of Apuleius and the Neo-Platonists, were no such holy, God-fearing spirits, but simply devils (ix, 18). Good angels have not the passions of men, nor the miseries of men, as these *daemones* have (ix, 6, 10, 16). Moreover, the word *daemon* is never used among us for a good angel (ix, 19).[1]

Chapters 13, 14, 15 of this ninth Book are an ingenious argumentation, which may be thus drawn out:

(*a*) God is happy and immortal.

(*b*) Man is miserable and mortal (c. 14).

(*c*) Platonic *daemones* are miserable and immortal (c. 13).

(*d*) Such *daemones* might conceivably serve as mediators between God and man, having with God one attribute, immortality, and with man also one attribute, misery.

(*e*) But their everlasting misery must come of sin of their own: since " as the world is ruled by Providence, not by chance, their misery would never be everlasting unless their wickedness were great " (c. 15).

(*f*) Such everlastingly miserable, wicked beings cannot be mediators between a good God and good men.

(*g*) Good angels, being happy and immortal, cannot be mediators between miserable, mortal man and a happy, immortal God (c. 15). As they are conjoined with God, so they are removed from men (c. 13).[2]

(*h*) The *one Mediator between God and man, the man Christ Jesus* (1 Tim. ii 5) had the attribute of immortality with God and as God, and the attribute of temporal misery with man: thus he, and he alone, was fitted to be Mediator (c. 15).

In ix, 14, 15, Augustine raises what he calls " a great question," whether man can be happy on earth; and rules it as " far more credible and probable that all men, so long as they are mortal, must be miserable." If by

[1] In classical Greek they spoke of ἀγαθὸς δαίμων, the " good genius," hence εὐδαίμων, " happy." But, standing by itself, the word δαίμων is used " more often of bad " than of good spirits (Liddell and Scott). In Aeschylus, *Agamemnon*, 1469, 1479, 1482, 1501, we have δαίμων identified with ἀλάστωρ, the evil genius of the family.

[2] But does not the Church invoke the intercession of the good angels ? Yes, but not as mediators of their own right and condition, but only through and in Jesus Christ.

" misery " is meant the absence of perfect happiness, the conclusion is clear, against the Stoics, whom St Augustine here confutes. But if " misery " means privation even of imperfect happiness, we may take this as an example of St Augustine's tendency to set extreme against extreme, overlooking all intermediate positions. Who has not enjoyed hours of quiet domestic happiness, happiness not, of course, absolute, happiness brief and fleeting, still very soothing so far as it went? One who knows something of Africa tells me he thinks there can have been very little even of that mild quality of happiness in the Africa of Augustine's day.[1]

In this Book Augustine quotes the greatest of the Neo-Platonists, Plotinus. Plotinus died A.D. 270, and is therefore later than Apuleius. Porphyry was his disciple. Plotinus is quoted as teaching that the souls of men departed become *daemones*, called in Latin *Lares* (household gods)—if they were good—so too Plato, *Republic*, v, 468-9; *Lemures*, or *Larvae* (ghosts, spectres), if they were wicked;[2] and *Manes* (simply shades), if they were betwixt and between. The use of these Latin designations argues that Augustine read his Plotinus in Latin.

[1] There are two exquisite pictures of earthly happiness in Newman. I quote *Sermon Notes*, p. 50: " Life was not a burden; it was dear to him; he enjoyed it; that he was unwilling to quit it was because he saw, he heard, etc.—his amusements, his pleasures; he went to his club, or to business, with his friends; he liked the warm fire, the light; he liked his family, home comforts, his dinner; he strolled out in summer, or he went to places of merry-making."

See, again, the description of " my friend Richard's " comfortable estate in *Historical Sketches*, quoted in Ward's *Life of Newman*, ii, 337.

[2] " Such an earthly soul is weighed down and dragged back again to the region of visibility, and goes hovering about tombs and graves. Such are the shadowy forms that are seen there in the shape of ghosts, souls not clean cut away from flesh, but partaking still of the visible, which is the reason that they are seen " (Plato, *Phaedo*, 81, C, D).

BOOK X

THE hero of this Book is Porphyry, as Varro, Apuleius, and Plotinus have been of Books preceding. Porphyry, A.D. 232-304, came from Tyre to Rome A.D. 262, studied three years under Plotinus, then spent the rest of his life in Sicily. From a phrase of St Augustine, "had you been a true lover of wisdom, you would not have been puffed up with vain science and shrunk (*resiluisses*) from the wholesome humility of Christ," it has been conjectured that he was for some time a Christian (*C. D.*, x, 28). He afterwards wrote a long work against the divinity of Christ, and is called by Augustine "a bitter enemy of Christians" (*C. D.*, xix, 22). As a philosopher his aim was *une œuvre de vulgarisation*, to make his master Plotinus intelligible to the multitude. He had a strong leaning to magic; from that, and from the place of his birth, Tyre or its neighbourhood, St Augustine calls him a Chaldean (*C. D.*, x, 10). He devotes to him a long chapter (*C. D.*, xix, 23).

Porphyry is not an interesting thinker, and his philosophy has fallen into the neglect which it deserves (Benn, *Greek Philosophers*, p. 574). It is not worth our while to wander through his ineptitudes, even with the wand of an Augustine to point them out. One topic may detain us, the pre-existence of the soul from eternity, which the Neo-Platonists taught. When confronted with the doctrine of their Master in the *Timaeus*, that the lesser deities were made by the one Supreme God, and that these inferior gods in their turn gave being to human souls, they escaped contradicting Plato by devising a distinction between a beginning in *time* and a beginning in *position*. "As," they said, "if a foot had been from eternity planted on the sand, the footprint would ever be beneath the foot that made it. None could doubt that the footprint had been made by him who trod there, and yet neither foot would be before footprint, nor footprint before foot, though the one had been made by the other." So, they went on to say, the world and the gods created therein have always existed, and he who made them has always existed, and yet they were made. This argument came to life again in the thirteenth century, when St Thomas argued the abstract philosophical possibility of a world created from eternity.

St Augustine continues insisting that to no angels, good or bad, are we to pay divine adoration, which he calls *latria*, a name that has become classical in our theology. The great act of *latria* is sacrifice. We must, then, sacrifice to God alone.

His temple we are all collectively and all individually: because he deigns to dwell in the harmonious assemblage of all, and at the same time to dwell in each. He is not greater in all together than he is in each; he is not susceptible of physical extension or division. When our heart is uplifted to him, our heart is his altar, his Only-begotten Son is the Priest through whom we appease him. We offer him sacrifices in blood, when we contend for truth even to the shedding of our blood. We burn before him sweet-smelling incense, when we are on fire with pious and holy love in his sight. To him we make vows and pay them, offering what are his gifts in us, even our own very selves. On solemn festivals and appointed days we dedicate and hallow the memory of his benefits, lest ingratitude and forgetfulness should creep in by lapse of time. To him we sacrifice a victim of humility and praise on the altar of our heart by the fire of fervent charity. To see him, as he is to be seen, and to cleave to him, we are cleansed from the stain of all sins and lustful desires, and consecrated in his Name. He is the source of our happiness, he is the end of all our desire. As for our final good, concerning which there is great discussion among philosophers, it is nothing else than to cleave to him. By his incorporeal embrace alone is the intellectual soul filled and fertilised with true [supernatural] virtues. This is the Good that we are bidden to *love with our whole heart, with our whole soul, with our whole strength.* To this Good we ought to be led by those by whom we are loved, and to lead to it those whom we love. Thus are fulfilled those *two commandments*, on which depend the *whole law and the prophets* (Mark xii 29-34) (*C.D.*, x, 3).

Before this Christian mysticism how pales the pseudo-mysticism of Porphyry and the Neo-Platonists!

After observing, in reference to angels, that "any immortal power which does not worship God is miserable, because deprived of God; and any that does worship God has no mind to be itself worshipped in God's stead," and quoting the text, *Any one sacrificing to gods shall be exterminated, except it be to the Lord alone* (Exod. xxii 20), St Augustine goes on to lay down the doctrine of sacrifice, at first vaguely and rhetorically, then more accurately, and ultimately by making all true and acceptable sacrifice to be part of that one great Sacrifice offered once for all on the Cross, and in its unity daily re-enacted on the Christian altar—the one Sacrifice of Christ and his Church, in which Sacrifice Christ is at once both Priest and Victim, and so is his Church also both Priest and Victim.

As for sacrifice, no man ever dares to say that it ought to be offered to any but God. Who has ever deemed it fit to sacrifice except to some being whom he either knew, or thought, or pretended to be God? . . . (c. 4). A true sacrifice is every work that is done to the end that we may cleave to God in holy fellowship; or in other words, every work that is referred to that Final Good whereby alone we can be truly happy [say, every supernatural work]. Hence a work of mercy done to man is not a sacrifice unless it be done for God. Sacrifice, though done or offered by man, is yet a divine thing, *res divina*, as the old Latins used to call it. Hence man's own person, consecrated to the name of God and devoted to God, inasmuch as he dies to the world to live to God,[1] is a sacrifice. *I pray you, brethren, offer your bodies a living sacrifice, holy, well-pleasing to God* (Rom. xii 1). If therefore the body, which the soul uses as an inferior

[1] Notice how death enters into sacrifice.

servant or instrument, is a sacrifice, when its good and right use is referred to God, how much more is the soul made a sacrifice, when she refers herself to God, is inflamed with his love, loses the form of secular desire, and is subjected and reformed to the immutable form of God, pleasing him by that which she has received of his bounty! Since, then, the works of mercy that we do to ourselves or to our neighbours, referring them to God, are true sacrifices; and works of mercy are done only for our deliverance from misery and thereby being made happy; and we are not happy except in that good of which it is said, *It is good for me to cleave to the Lord* (Ps. 72); it follows beyond all doubt that the whole redeemed City, the congregation and fellowship of Saints, is offered as a universal sacrifice to God by the High Priest, who in the form of a servant has offered himself in his Passion for us that we might be members of so venerable a Head. This *form of a servant* (Phil. ii 7) it was that he offered, in this was he offered, because in this respect he is Mediator; in this, Priest; in this, Sacrifice. According to the Apostle (Rom. xii 1-5), this whole sacrifice, of which he speaks, we ourselves are. This is the sacrifice of Christians, *many one body in Christ*. And this the Church re-enacts (*frequentat*) in the Sacrament of the Altar known to the faithful, to the end that it may be shown to her that in the oblation which she offers she herself is offered (*C. D.*, x, 6).

Are we listening to a Father of the fifth century or to the Council of Trent, Sess. 22? And further—to bring together old and new in what is ever one and the same Church—we find here the essential groundwork of the devotion known to Catholics as the Morning Offering of the Apostleship of Prayer. St Augustine completes his doctrine of sacrifice:

The true Mediator, the man Christ Jesus, took the form of a servant, and therein was made Mediator between God and mankind. In the form of God he receives sacrifice along with the Father, with whom he is one God; but in the form of a servant he has preferred to be the sacrifice rather than receive it, lest he should give occasion for anyone to think it right to sacrifice to any creature. Thereby also is he a priest, himself the offerer, himself also the oblation. Of this truth he has wished there to be a daily sacred sign (*sacramentum*) in the sacrifice of the Church, which being the Body whereof he is the Head, learns to offer herself through him. The ancient sacrifices of the saints were manifold and various signs of this true sacrifice. And to this supreme and true sacrifice all false sacrifices have given place.

A word on the theology of the Mass will go to make all this clear. In the Mass there is one chief priest, who is also chief Victim; and one subsidiary priest, who is likewise subsidiary victim. The chief Priest is our Saviour Jesus Christ, offering himself, his own Body and Blood, by that self-same one act of sacrifice whereby he offered himself on the Cross; for, as the Council of Trent teaches (Sess. 22), the Mass is one sacrifice with the sacrifice of the Cross, only the manner of offering being different. The subsidiary priest is the Church, represented by the duly ordained mortal man who says the Mass, and by all the faithful present who hear the Mass, and offer it along with him and through his ministry, *meum ac vestrum sacrificium*. The Church, the priest offering and the faithful present, are also the subsidiary victim, being offered body and soul to God along with the Body and Blood of their Mediator and Head, whose members they are. This offering of themselves is an exercise of that *holy priesthood*, that *royal priesthood* (1 Pet. ii 5, 9) which belongs to all the faithful as such.

Taken in its context, then, St Augustine's saying is theologically accurate: " A true sacrifice is every work that is done to the end that we may cleave to God in holy fellowship." In other words, every supernatural act, done by a member of the Church in the state of grace, is part of the Great Sacrifice of Christ and his Church.

In xvi, 22, he observes of the sacrifice of Melchisedech: " There the sacrifice first appeared, which is now offered to God by Christians all the world over."

And again (xvii, 20) on the text, *There is no good for a man but what he shall eat and drink* (Eccles. ii 24), " What more credible meaning is there than a reference to the partaking of this table, which Christ himself, Mediator of the New Covenant and Priest according to the order of Melchisedech, sets forth of his own Body and Blood? In place of all those sacrifices and oblations of the Old Testament his Body is offered, and ministered to them that partake." The application of the text of Ecclesiastes is questionable, but beyond question Augustine was a "massing priest."

BOOK XI

THE preceding ten Books represent four years' labour of the Bishop of Hippo. We are come now to the year A.D. 417. There are twelve more Books to write, and it will take nine years to write them. In them the author will narrate the origin, history, and final end of the Two Cities, beginning with the creation and fall of the angels, and ending with the Day of Judgement. For this *Histoire Universelle* the chief authority is Scripture; the work, therefore, assumes the character of a running commentary on the Old Testament.

And, first, Augustine is taken up with the vast consideration, that has occupied so many minds since, of the eternity that was ere the world was created, and of the infinite space that is where the world is not. The world was created, we will say, x million years ago: x is an unknown quantity, enormous, but still finite, if the world began in time at all. Run back in thought the whole length of x, and where are you? You have got to the anterior limit of time; there is no time beyond that; the world and time began together, for time is "the number of motion"; no motion, no time; and when the world is not, there can be no motion; for there is nothing to move, only the unchangeable God.

Again, though Augustine does not notice this, the universe as a whole is probably in motion; what is the space interminable through which it moves?

This speculation occupies xi, 4, 5, 6. The point which Augustine seems to make is this:

If they say that the thoughts of men are idle, whereby infinite places are imagined, since there is no place but the world, they are met with the answer that at that rate it is idle to think of past times when God was doing nothing, since there is no time before the world.

Certainly no time, χρόνος, before the world; and no *place*, τόπος, but that which is occupied by the world; but for *eternity*, αἰών, the world was not, and through infinite *space* (χώρα, *room*) the world probably is moving. Mysteries remain.

There is a happy phrase in the opening of this Book which the reader should not miss:

The one thoroughly laid down and safe way (*via munitissima*) to avoid all going wide of truth is the doctrine of the Incarnation—that one and the same person is God and man; as God, the end of our going; as man, the way we are to go (*ut idem ipse sit Deus et homo, quo itur Deus, qua itur homo*) (xi, 2).

No neater, more complete and accurate statement of the Incarnation could anywhere be found.

Finding no other mention of the creation of the angels in Genesis, St Augustine takes *Let there be light* (Gen. i 3) to signify that creation, and the *separation of light from darkness* to be the divine foreknowledge of what angels would persevere in good and who would not (xi, 9, 19). Here, then, in the first three verses of the Bible, we have the original foundation and separation of the Two Cities.

In xi, 18, St Augustine starts an idea which goes as far towards the solution of the problem of evil as human intellect can travel in the wake of that inscrutable mystery, the idea of the *beauty* of the universe consisting in the *harmony of opposites*.

For God would not create, I do not say of angels, but even of men, any individual whom he foresaw would be evil, unless he foresaw all along to what uses of his good servants he would apply these his evil servants, and so adorn the order of the ages like a beautiful poem (*pulcerrimum carmen*) with antitheses. This is most clearly expressed in the Book of Ecclesiasticus (xxxiii 15): *Against evil is good, and against death life, so against the pious man the sinner. And so look upon all the works of the Most High, two and two, one against one.*

" Antitheses " (*antitheta*), Augustine explains, is a rhetorical term, which he illustrates from 2 Cor. vi 7-10. St Thomas says that what God cares most for in creation is " the beauty of the universe," in this Augustinian sense.[1]

Here is a notable utterance on the Ideal Order of possible creations:

There are not many wisdoms, or orders of truth; there is but one wisdom, one order of truth; and in that there are immense and unchangeable treasures of things intelligible, including all invisible and unchangeable ideals (*rationes*), even of things visible and changeable which by this wisdom are made.[2] It cannot rightly be said of any human artist that he works blindly; neither has God wrought anything in ignorance of what he was making. He has made all things with knowledge: things that he knew beforehand, such things he has made. Hereupon occurs a thought, wonderful but true; this world could not be known to us unless it existed; but it could not exist unless it were known beforehand to God (*C. D.*, xi, 10).

On the text, *From the beginning the devil sinneth*, some have argued that sin is natural to the devil; but if natural, it can be no sin. " He is not to be thought to have sinned from the beginning of his creation, but from the beginning of his sin, because sin began with his pride " (xi, 15). The text simply means that the devil was the first sinner.

Things higher in the scale are not thereby always preferable morally and practically. " Who would not rather have bread in his house than mice ? Though in the order of nature angels stand higher than men, yet by the law

[1] *Contra Gentiles*, ii, 45, *n*. 7; iii, 71, 94. See notes to my Translation, pp. 242, 255.

[2] The reader who does not understand this pregnant sentence should get hold of some Catholic manual of logic and metaphysics, and study there the doctrine of things possible, also the thesis that the intelligible essences of things are unchangeable and eternal. This is the truth of Platonic Ideas, or Ideals.

of justice good men are preferred to bad angels" (c. 16). And good Catholic laymen to bad schismatic priests.

The following throws light on St Augustine's method of interpreting Scripture:

> We have in mind two societies of angels, one enjoying God, the other swollen with pride; one to whom it is said, *Adore him, all ye angels* (Ps. xcvi 7), the other whose chief says, *All these things will I give thee, if thou wilt fall down and adore me* (Matt. iv 9); one on fire with the holy love of God, the other reeking with the unclean love of its own excellence; and since, as it is written, *God resisteth the proud, but giveth grace to the humble* (Jas. iv 6), the one dwelling in the heaven of heavens, the other thence cast down and making turmoil in this lower air; the one in the bright calm of devotion, the other overclouded with unholy desires; the one, as God bids, rendering kindly succour or wreaking just vengeance, the other boiling over with proud ambition to subdue and wild craving to do hurt; the one the minister of God's goodness in taking care of men so far as he wills, the other restrained by God's power from doing all the hurt they wish. These, then, are the two societies of angels, unlike and contrary to one another; the one good by nature, and right of will; the other also good by nature, but perverse of will. Besides more manifest testimonies of Scripture in which their characters are set forth, they are also denoted in this book of Genesis by the names of *light* and *darkness*. So we have thought, though it may be that the writer had something else in his mind in this passage (*aliud sensit qui scripsit*). Our discussion of the obscurity of the phrase has not been useless. Even though we have not been able to search out what the author of this book wanted to say, still we have not wandered from the rule of faith, sufficiently well known to the faithful by other sacred writings of the same authority. Granting even that it is the material works of God that are referred to here, still such material things have doubtless a likeness to spiritual things, as the Apostle says: *All ye are children of the light and sons of the day; we are not of the night nor of darkness* (1 Thess. v 5). But if it be that this was also the sense of the writer, all the better for the purpose of our argument (*C. D.*, xi, 33).

Theologically we observe here:

(*a*) St Augustine does not distinguish the literal sense,

intended by the Holy Ghost, from the *accommodated* sense, not so intended. It is enough for the *accommodated* sense " not to wander from the rule of faith "; for the *literal*, as also for the *mystical* sense, it is further necessary not to wander beyond the inspired meaning of the passage.

(*b*) In terms of modern theology, what St Augustine says comes to this: " Light and darkness may be taken for good and bad angels, at least in an *accommodated* sense: if that is the *literal* sense, all the better for me."

(*c*) No argument can be drawn from the *accommodated* sense of Scripture. This St Augustine himself virtually allows in *C. D.*, xvii, 15.

Side by side with Genesis i 12, 18, 21, 25, 31, *And God saw that it was good*, St Augustine sets Plato's saying in the *Timaeus*, 37 D: " And when the Father who begat it perceived the created image of the eternal gods, that it had motion and life, he rejoiced and was well pleased." He goes on:

> Plato was not so foolish as to suppose God made happier by the knowledge of his work, but he wished to signify that the same work pleased the Artificer, when done, which had pleased him as a work of art to do, not that God's knowledge changes in any way, as though things not yet done, or being done, or already done, impress him differently; his knowledge is not couched in three tenses, nor does the aspect of his mind pass from thought to thought (xi, 21).

The above is an elementary and axiomatic truth of theology, and must be held, if we are to have any concept worthy of God at all.

The following may have suggested to Descartes his celebrated *cogito*, *ergo sum*. But the Cartesian philosophy must not be fathered on St Augustine. He writes against the Academic school of sceptics:

> We are, and we know that we are, and we love that being and knowledge. On those three facts no possible likeness of falsehood to truth troubles us. We do not touch them by any bodily sense, as we feel colours by sight, sounds by

hearing, odours by smelling, hardness and softness by handling. Of such sensible objects we form images resembling them, images no longer corporeal. These images we turn over in thought, hold to them by memory, and by them are roused to desire of their objects. But without any imagination, or sport of fancy, I am most certain that I am, that I know that I am, and love my being. On these truths I dread no arguments of Academics, saying, " What if you are mistaken ?" For if I am mistaken, I am in being. He that is not cannot be mistaken, and if I am mistaken, by that very fact I exist. He who is not in existence surely cannot be mistaken; and if I am mistaken, by that very fact I am an existent being.

BOOK XII

THERE are not Four Cities: good angels, good men; evil angels, evil men; but Two Cities: good angels and men, evil angels and men. For there is one common principle, common to angels and men—one principle of good and evil, and finally of happiness or misery. That principle is " cleaving to God " (*adhaerere Deo*), or, the alternative, " standing off from God," and making one's final end oneself.

Some (angels and men alike) steadily set up their rest in the good that is common to them all, in God himself, his eternity, truth, love. Other (angels and men) choose rather to delight in their own power, as though they were their own sufficient good, and so have drifted away from the higher general good and source of happiness to purposes of their own. They have taken the pomp of pride for the height of eternity, empty deceit for certain truth, party-spirit for undivided charity; and so have become proud, deceitful, envious beings. If it is asked why the one are happy, the right answer is, " because they cleave to God." If it is asked why the other are miserable, the right answer is, " because they do not cleave to God." There is no good capable of making any rational or intellectual creature happy except God (xii, 1).

We have in such words as these the backbone of the *De Civitate Dei*, the characteristic mark of the one City and the other, the gist and essence of the differentiation—so detested by the World—of Heaven and Hell. We cannot here call St Augustine antiquated. He brings us here up against the truth, which of all truths is the first that needs instilling into the modern mind, which complains that it cannot see its way to any religion: *Self, holding on to God, is happiness, wisdom, heaven; self, breaking away from God, is misery, folly, hell.*

We have seen that *Deitas* was a new-coined word in St Augustine's age: so also was *essentia*. He says: " As from *sapere* we have *sapientia*, so from *esse* we have *essentia*, a new name that the old Latin authors did not use, but which has come into use in our time, that our language might not be wanting in an equivalent for *οὐσία* " (c. 2; *cf. De moribus Manichaeorum*, ii, cap. 2). He argues, as often against the Manichees, that as to *esse* (being) there is no positive contrary, but only the sheer negation, *not-being*, so " to God, the supreme essence and author of all essences, there is no contrary essence,"—no sheer evil positively standing out against the Absolute Goodness of God; all evil is a flaw (*vitium*) in some nature, of itself good (xii, 2, 3; xi, 17). Things irrational are good in themselves, though they often get in our way and thwart our purpose; they are part of the beauty of the universe, and so of the praise of the Creator. The only thing that really makes against God is an evil will, whether of angels or men; now an evil will is not an *efficient*, but a *deficient* cause; it is idle to look for any efficient cause of deficiency. St Thomas, *Contra Gentiles*, iii, 10, follows up this argument to greater subtlety; all sin is *acting inconsiderately;* the mere failure of consideration is indeed not a sin, nor any positive act or cause whatever, but it is the occasion of all sin. Man is by nature liable to sin, defectible, *changeable;* so he must be, because he is *made out of nothing*, and he cannot be otherwise than made out of nothing. God alone is by nature *unchangeable* in good. If the blessed in heaven are so unchangeable, it is not of themselves, but by their participation in God. St Augustine is fond of this argument (cc. 6, 7, 8).

In this chapter (xii, 6) St Augustine states exactly the position of free will:

If two men are attacked by the same temptation, and one yields to it and consents, the other, having been antecedently in the same position, stands out, what is the evident truth but this, that the one *willed*, the other *willed not*, to fall away from chastity? Whence but by each one's own will, where there was antecedently the same affection of body and mind in both?

It was a common opinion among the ancient Greeks and Egyptians, that the human race has always been on earth, but has been periodically swept away by deluges and conflagrations, and started afresh. Some philosophers made a sort of recurring decimal of universal history, as though periodically the universe fell back into a previous state, and then repeated all its past development. (See Virgil, *Ecl.*, iv, 34-6, and the mythus in Plato's *Politicus*, pp. 270 *seq.*) Against this, Augustine argues (xii, 10, 11, 13). He says: "They say what they think, not what they know." Our physicists and geologists have swept away the entire speculation. The world of matter and sense cannot have been from eternity, or its energy would have been all dissipated ere now; and once run down, we see no way how the cosmic clockwork could ever have wound itself up again. Nor, of course, has this globe always been habitable, nor will it be for ever an apt dwelling-place for man.

C. 15 is characteristically Augustinian. He resumes the difficulty of x, 31; xi, 4, 5: how creation can have been otherwise than from eternity. He says at the end of c. 14: "It is a very deep matter of thought, that God has existed from eternity, and at some definite date (*ex aliquo tempore*) first willed to create man, whom he had never made, and yet never changed his purpose and will." The answer now given in the schools is that the purpose was from eternity, to take effect, as it did take effect, at the beginning of time. But behind that there lies this further difficulty: how came God, having from eternity a purpose to create, and therefore ultimately actually creating, be in himself exactly the same unchangeable God as he would have been, and might have been (for creation is no necessity of his nature, but a free act) had he chosen to forego all creation, and live in eternal solitude alone by himself? Let us hear St Augustine:

> I fear I may be more readily judged to be asserting what I do not know than to be teaching what I do know. I return, therefore, to things that our Creator has wished us to know; as for other things which he has permitted wiser men than me to know in this life, or has absolutely reserved for the perfect to know in another life, I confess they are beyond my powers. But I have thought it right to treat these matters without affirming anything, that readers may see from what dangerous questions they ought to refrain, and not think themselves capable of everything, but rather recognise the wholesomeness of obedience to the Apostle's precept (Rom. xii 3). If an infant is fed according to its strength, it will grow and take in more; but if it goes beyond the powers of its capacity, it will die ere ever it grows (c. 15).

The precise difficulty before which St Augustine recoils is this: how can God have been from eternity Lord, if there have not been from eternity creatures for him to lord it over? In his treatise *On the Trinity*, which he was writing simultaneously with the *City of God*, St Augustine answers this difficulty very sufficiently. Why in the one work he does not refer to the other, we do not know. The answer, given in *De Trinitate*, v, c. 16, admits that God has been lord only since creation began, but denies that this new denomination makes any change in God. The argument, if admitted, he says, would prove too much. It would prove that I individually must have been from eternity; for God is not only Lord in general of all creation, he is also in particular *my Lord.* The solution all lies in this sentence: " God's beginning in time to be called what he was not called before, is manifestly a temporal denomination (*manifestum est relative dici*), not implying any accident in God, as though anything happened to him, but decidedly implying accident in that in relation to which God begins to have some denomination." When the just man begins (in baptism) to be the friend of God, it is the man that is changed, not God. This truth is expressed by the scholastic thesis, that while creatures are *really* related to God, God is not related to creatures *really*, but *conceptionally* only. We cannot but think of him as really related to us, though he is not so; our inability to think otherwise is part of the incomprehensibility of the Absolute in our regard. Suarez (*Metaphysics*, *disp*. 30, *sect*. 9, *n*. 4) remarks mildly: " This is one of the darker questions in theology." Beyond a certain limit, the darkness is impenetrable, as St Augustine says.[1]

The following is significant in view of the Great War, 1914-18:

> Nor was God ignorant that man would sin, and that mortal men would go so far on their monstrous course of sinning that beasts devoid of rational will would live together according to their kind on a footing of greater peace and security than men; for never have lions or dragons waged such wars with one another as men with men.

He goes on to say that God foresaw on the other side the eternal peace of his elect (c. 22).

The book closes with the words:

> From the first man were to come men of future time, some to be associated with the evil angels in punishment, some with the good angels in reward, and that by a judgement of God, secret but still just. For whereas it is written: *All the ways of the Lord are mercy and truth* (Ps. xxiv 10), neither can his grace be unjust, nor his justice cruel (*nec injusta ejus gratia, nec crudelis potest esse justitia*) (c. 27).

[1] More of this in my work published by Longmans, *Studies in God and His Creatures*, pp. 92-108.

BOOK XIII

DEATH for Adam's sin is the subject of this Book. In reading it, and the Book that follows, on Concupiscence, one general observation may be attended to. Augustine knew, but never held steadily before his mind, the fact that death and concupiscence are *natural* to man in virtue of the animal nature which he has in common with the lower animals; that Adam's original exemption therefrom was a gratuitous boon, not due to his nature; that what mankind lost in Adam was this and other gratuitous boons, not anything that our nature, as such, has a claim to (*e.g.*, some final natural happiness); consequently, that death and concupiscence in our present state are no malignant growths upon our nature, but things of themselves incident to that same nature, and therefore not by strict definition *evils*, since they are no privation of anything due to the constitution of man as man. In calling a thing *natural*, I take St Augustine's own definition of nature: " Nature is nothing else than that which a thing is understood to be in its own kind " (*De moribus Manichaeorum*, ii, cap. 2). By that definition we do right in speaking of dying as " paying the debt of nature."

Augustine's whole career shows us what it is for a genius and a saint to be his own professor. Augustine never sat on the benches in any school of theology. Indeed, the school of theology can hardly be said to have existed in his day. He was a founder of the school, a pioneer of theology; no wonder if he lost his bearings sometimes. No pioneer is apt always to see his way clearly.

It is the death of the soul, when God forsakes it; as it is the death of the body, when the soul forsakes it. Therefore it is the death of both, that is, of the whole man, when the soul, forsaken of God, forsakes the body. The authority of Holy Writ (Apoc. xxxi 8) calls that the *second death*" (xiii, 2).

As for the first death, that of the body, it may be said that it is good for the good, evil for the evil; but as for the second, as no good man dies that death, so for none is it good so to die (xiii, 2).

But Augustine will not allow that death is good, even for the good.

As for the death of the body, or the separation of the soul from the body, it is good for no man. It is a rough, painful, and unnatural violence, that tears asunder two elements that had been knit and joined together in the living man (xiii, 6).

But surely, when the body is no longer *in potentia ad vitam*, no longer apt matter for the soul to inform and vivify, is there anything unnatural in the soul leaving it? And is our body by nature made so strong as to be able to afford a perpetual footing for the soul?

It seems largely a matter of words whether we choose to say that death is natural, part of the course of nature, and therefore not evil; or unnatural, breaking up nature, and so evil. Perhaps the case is best put as St Augustine first put it, *bonis bona*, *malis mala*. Augustine, however, prefers to say that "as evil men put the law to evil use, though the law is good (Rom. vii 12, 13), so the good die well, though death is an evil" (c. 5). In c. 11 death is considered somewhat as Horatio says to Hamlet "too curiously."

Augustine had a controversial interest in insisting on the evil of death rather than on its good. First there was the then rising heresy of Pelagius, which made light of Adam's sin and all its consequences. Then there were the Platonists. The Platonic philosophy, widening even to dualism the relation of soul to body, as though it were that of a bird in a cage, eulogised death as a deliverance. Confronted with Christianity, the Neo-Platonists ridiculed the doctrines of death being the punishment of Adam's sin, and of the final resurrection of the body. Augustine (c. 16) replies *ad hominem*, not very happily, that Plato in the *Timaeus* assigns bodies to the inferior gods, and promises perpetual union of the spirits with those bodies as a blessing. It is obvious that the bodies in question were not human bodies, such as ours; Plato was thinking chiefly of the stars, which he took to be animate. As to the animation of the stars, Augustine declines to pronounce (c. 17). As for the resurrection, we may allow to Platonists and others that it would be a very questionable benefit for a soul to be brought back, as the Platonic doctrine of transmigration supposed, to the animal, mortal body such as ours is now; but the body of the just in the resurrection will be spiritual and immortal, as St Paul says (1 Cor. xv 44, 53). And if you ask me how a human body can be made spiritual and immortal, I tell you roundly, I do not know. Neither do you know anything to the contrary. Your limited human experience does not warrant your setting limits to the Creator's power. For the realisation of happiness it is not necessary to eschew everything corporeal, but only bodies corruptible, troublesome, burdensome, moribund, such as the goodness of God did not make for the first men, but the punishment of sin compelled (c. 17). And the bodies of the just in the resurrection shall be far more glorious than the bodies of Adam and Eve in Paradise (c. 20). "They shall be *spiritual*, not that they shall cease to be bodies, but because a quickening spirit shall be the principle of their subsistence (*spiritu vivificante subsistent*) (c. 22)—a remark that will bear development.

Some writers, as Philo, and possibly Origen, wished to take the whole description of the Earthly Paradise for a pure allegory. Augustine shows how it is capable of allegorical interpretation, but he adds: "Still we must believe in the most faithful truth and historical character of the narrative" (c. 21; *cf.* xv, 27). And such has ever been the attitude of the Church towards the Old Testament narratives. There is continual allegory, as St Augustine is always insisting; there is also historical truth, and the Church would have us insist on the production of proof positive before we allow any of these narratives to be mere allegory and no history at all. We may compare the history and the allegory to a distant range of mountains covered with clouds. It is often difficult to say what is mountain and what is cloud. But the "seated hills" are there; it is not all "the baseless fabric of a vision," mere cloud-bank and Oriental imagery. And in particular the fall of our first parents is a fact of history.

BOOK XIV

THIS Book deals with the passions let loose in man by Adam's sin, passions whereof he had a control which we through him have lost. Much of the argument will be found in St Augustine's Antipelagian treatise *De nuptiis et concupiscentia.* He begins with once more differentiating the Two Cities, the Elect and the Reprobate. In consequence of Adam's sin, he says, " The kingdom of death dominated mankind to such an extent as to drive all, by due penalty, headlong into the second death, of which there is no end, except that the undue grace of God has delivered some." This sentence, penned some time before A.D. 420, is the germ of the Augustinian theory of predestination, which reached its full development seven years later in the *De correptione et gratia.* Hence, he goes on, notwithstanding all the varieties of mankind, we distribute the entire race adequately into these Two Cities, one living according to the flesh, the other according to the spirit (xiv, 1). *The flesh* in this phrase does not simply mean *the body.* It was an error of the Platonists—and of the Manichees, who erred here more grievously still—to put down all a man's evil doings to his body (c. 5). Satan has no body, and yet he is the arch-sinner. There are spiritual as well as carnal sins, sins Satanic as well as sins bestial; all of them *works of the flesh.* So St Paul, among such works, enumerates *idolatries, poisonings, enmities, contentions, heresies* (Gal. v 20). To live *according to the flesh* is to live *according to man,* and not that simply, but according to man separating himself and making himself independent of God (cc. 3, 4).

There follows a discussion on the passions, a celebrated

theme of dispute between Stoic and Peripatetic (xiv, 8, 9, resuming ix, 4, 5). St Augustine, and the Church with him, is against the Stoics, who would root out emotion entirely.

And if some [*i.e.*, the Stoic philosophers] with a vanity all the more monstrous for its being so rare, have made it their hobby never to be roused and excited, bent or inclined by any emotion, they are in a way rather to lose all humanity than to attain to true tranquillity. For a policy is not right by the mere fact of its being hard, nor sound by the fact of its being unfeeling (*non enim quia durum aliquid, ideo rectum; aut quia stupidum est, ideo sanum*) (xiv 9):

which last sentence might have served as book-mark for the Abbé Saint-Cyran in his readings of St Augustine.

Then of Adam's sin (cc. 11, 12). God's counsel was not thereby upset: he foresaw it, and saw and willed what good could be made out of that evil. It was a great evil, because it was a great disobedience; Adam was so much stronger to obey, if he would, than we are. *Adam was not deceived* (1 Tim. ii 14) by the serpent; he sinned solely because he was unwilling to dissociate himself from the one companion he had; still he sinned with full advertence, except perhaps that he did not expect the divine judgement on his sin to be so severe. Adam yielded to his wife, as Solomon to his wives (3 Kings xi 4), and Aaron to the people (Exod. xxxii 1-6), seeing the folly of it all the while. " Whoever thinks this condemnation (of Adam) excessive or unjust, certainly does not know the iniquity there was in sinning where there was such facility for not sinning " (c. 15) He contrasts Adam's wanton disobedience with Abraham's hard obedience over the sacrifice of Isaac. Adam's sin is a typical instance of the sin that divides the City of the Reprobate from the City of the Just, to wit, pride, self-pleasing, revolt from God.

The virtue that is specially commended to the City of God, at present in pilgrimage in this world; the virtue that is specially panegyrised in Christ its King, is humility; the vice contrary to this virtue, elation of heart, is predominant in the devil, its adversary; this, then, is the great differentiating mark whereby City is marked off from City, the society of pious men from the impious, with the angels severally belonging to each; love of God leads in the one, self-love in the other.

In xii, 6, St Augustine gave what we may call the natural, psychological definition of free will. Here he gives another, and it is his favourite definition: " The freedom of the will is then true freedom, when it does not serve vices and sins." And he quotes John viii 34-36 (*cf.* Rom. vi 16 *seq.*): *If the Son shall set you free, ye shall then be truly free.* By *true* is here meant " profitable to eternal salvation," as when Augustine speaks of " true " in opposition to more natural virtues. Free will may be turned to sin; indeed, nothing can be a sin that is not an act of free will; but there is always an element of the irrational, the inconsiderate, the wayward, the arbitrary and enslaving, in every sinful act. The highest and most godlike liberty is to rise in full intelligence above sin (c. 11).

Adam's disobedience was punished in him and his posterity by that disobedience of appetite to reason which is called " concupiscence " (cc. 16-20). In paradise, there would have been intercourse of the sexes without concupiscence or lust; so St Augustine (cc. 22-26). St John Chrysostom, following Origen, held that there would have been no intercourse of the sexes there at all; but that is not the common opinion. If Adam and Eve had not sinned, mankind would have been left in Paradise, availing themselves of the blessing, *Increase and multiply* (Gen. i 28) " until the number of the predestined was made up: then a still greater beatitude would have been bestowed on them, the same as is given to the blessed angels " (xiv, 10).

The last chapter of this Book (xiv, 28) contains the celebrated words, already quoted, descriptive of the Two Cities as made by two loves: *fecerunt Civitates duas amores duo.*

We must not pass over the chapter (xiv, 26) where St Augustine rises to his height, describing the earthly paradise:

> Man then lived in paradise as he would, so long as he would have what God had ordered. He lived enjoying God, enjoying the Good whereby he was good; he lived without any want, having it in his power so to live always. There was food at hand to keep him from hunger, drink to keep off thirst, the tree of life to prevent the wasting away of old age. Nothing of corruption in his body or from his body caused any annoyance to any of his senses. There was no fear of disease within, nor of any blow from without. Perfect soundness in his flesh, entire tranquillity in his soul. As in the garden there was no heat or cold, so in his dwelling there was no hindrance to good will from any cupidity or fear. There was no breath of sadness, nor any folly of mirth, but true joy perpetuated from God. *Charity from a pure heart and a good conscience and faith unfeigned* (1 Tim. i 5) set him on fire with love of God. His conjugal state was one of faithful, virtuous love. His mind and body kept watch in harmony together. The keeping of the commandment cost him no trouble.

And yet man did not do well in those fair surroundings. Was it that there was nothing about them of the Cross?

BOOK XV

THE next two Books (XV, XVI) are a running commentary on Genesis. Then one Book (XVII) on the time of the Hebrew Kings, and one (XVIII) on the history of the Gentile world. Universal history is not apt to be a happy undertaking, as St Augustine found. These four Books will seem to some readers the least satisfactory in the whole work. They are meant to be a history of the Two Cities—*i.e.*, a history of mankind up to the coming of Christ. He sees the Two Cities in Cain and Abel, in Cham and Sem, in Ismael and Isaac, in Esau and Jacob, in the Deluge and the Ark. The citizen of the City of God is "predestined by grace, elect by grace, by grace a pilgrim below, by grace a citizen above. So far as he himself is concerned, he comes of the same lump of clay (*massa*) as other men, and that clay was originally all condemned; but God, as a potter, out of the same clay *has made one vessel to honour, another to dishonour* (Rom. ix 21). It is not every bad man that will ever be good, but there will be no good man who was not at some time bad; but the quicker one turns to the better [*i.e.*, is baptised], the sooner he is named after the grace that he has attained to, and by his new name covers his old" (xv, 1).

The Earthly City is temporal only; it will be no City in the next world, where it is given over to punishment. On earth it is divided against itself, and torn with wars. Peace on earth, when found, is a common good of both Cities.

This peace is sought after by laborious wars, and attained by what is accounted glorious victory. When victory falls to the side that had the juster cause for fighting, who doubts that such victory is matter of congratulation, and the peace that has come of it desirable? Such victory and peace are good things, and beyond doubt are gifts of God. But if the better gifts are neglected, that belong to the City that is above, where there shall be victory secure in everlasting and perfect peace; if instead of better things these temporal gifts are desired, and believed to be the only good gifts, or are loved more than gifts which are believed to be better, then new misery must ensue, and old wounds break out (xv, 4).

This is St Augustine's word for "after the war" (1914-18). We may pass over the rest of this Book. The difficulties of the narrative of Genesis are well known. Augustine discusses them profusely, but really, for a modern reader, effects little towards their removal.

In xv, 27 he discusses the storage of the Ark. We must remember that the Ark was not a ship, but a floating magazine, a three-decker. The "cubit" is an uncertain measure, but, taking it at 21 inches, the dimensions of the Ark work out approximately, 525 feet long, 87 feet broad, 52 feet high. The *Lusitania* was 762 by 75 by 56 feet. The *Titanic* 850 by 92 by 64 feet.

BOOK XVI

TREATING of the mystical sense of the Old Testament, this Book runs parallel with Books XII and XXII against Faustus the Manichee.

No plainer case of an Old Testament narrative bearing a mystical sense can be found than the sacrifice of Abraham (Gen. xxii).

In a series of events too long to dwell upon we come to the temptation of Abraham in the immolation of his beloved son Isaac, a trial of his religious obedience, destined to make it known to ages to come, not to God. Not every temptation is to be imputed to a fault: the temptation whereby is made probation is matter of congratulation. Generally there is no other way for a human soul to come to know herself than by answering to herself what her powers are, not by word, but by experience, the temptation, as it were, putting the question. If there she recognises the gift of God, then she is pious, then she is solidly established in the sure strength of grace, not puffed up by empty boasting. Abraham could never have believed that God took delight in human sacrifices; but, when the divine command thundered in his ear, he had to obey, not to dispute. Still Abraham is to be quoted as having believed that his son would rise again after immolation, for God had said to him, *In Isaac shall thy seed be called* (Gen. xxi 12; Heb. xi 18); where the text runs on, *whence also he received him in likeness*. In likeness of what? Of that whereof the same Apostle says: *Who spared not his only-begotten Son, but gave him up for us all* (Rom. viii 32). Therefore also, as the Lord carried his cross, so Isaac himself bore to the place of sacrifice the wood on which he was to be laid. Lastly, what was that ram by the immolation of which the sacrifice was completed in mystic blood? The ram was held fast by its horns in a bush. Who else was figured thereby than Jesus, who before his immolation was crowned with Jewish[1] thorns? (xix, 32).

[1] Surely Roman thorns, but Jewish ill-treatment.

The mystical sense is not always so clear and striking; but one clear example shows that the mystical sense exists. Another example (c. 35) is that of Jacob and Esau struggling for birth (Gen. xxv 22-23), applied by St Paul (Rom. ix 10-13).

Christ is in the blessing that Isaac invoked on Jacob (Gen. xxvii 27-29): "With the odour of the name of Christ, like a field, the world is filled; his is the blessing from the dew of heaven, that is, from the rain of divine words; and from the abundance of earth, that is from the gathering of peoples: his is the abundance of corn and wine, that is, the multitude which the corn and wine gathers together in the Sacrament of his Body and Blood" (c. 37).

In xvi, 10, the existence of Antipodes is pronounced quite incredible, on the ground that Adam's descendants could never have crossed the ocean and got there.

We may observe that the word *Hebrew* represents περάτης, "the man who has come *across* from abroad," a name given to Abraham (Gen. xxiii 4); it has nothing to do with Heber (Gen. x 24-25). Abraham did not speak Hebrew, still less did Heber (c. 11); Hebrew is not the original language spoken before the confusion of tongues (Gen. xi; c. 11). Errors of this kind are not to be imputed to St Augustine, but to the age in which he lived.

BOOK XVII

C.3 IS a valuable summing up of St Augustine's whole doctrine on the literal and the mystical sense of the Old Testament.

There are found three kinds of utterances of the Prophets: some refer to the earthly Jerusalem, some to the heavenly, some to both. I see I must prove what I say by examples. The prophet Nathan was sent to rebuke David for a grave sin, and to foretell evils to come which actually did ensue (2 Kings [Sam.] xii). Who can doubt that such dealings, whether in public or private life, belonged to the earthly City? But where it is read, *Lo, the days are coming when I will conclude for the house of Israel and the house of Juda a new covenant*, etc. (Jerem. xxxi 31-41; Heb. viii 8-12), beyond doubt the subject of such a prophecy is the heavenly Jerusalem, of which God himself is the reward. To both the one and the other belong the circumstance of Jerusalem being called the city of God, and the house of God therein foretold, which prophecy seems to be fulfilled in the building of that famous temple of Solomon. The building of it was an event in the history of the earthly Jerusalem, and a figure of the heavenly. Some have thought that there is nothing in the books of the Old Testament, no prophecy, no event, that does not imply something belonging to the heavenly City, and its children, pilgrims in this life. In that case there will be no detail referring to the earthly Jerusalem only. But in my opinion they on the one hand are very much mistaken who think that nothing in that history has any other signification except what is related to have happened there and then; on the other hand, they are very bold who contend that absolutely everything there is wrapped up in allegorical meanings. Still, what faithful man can doubt that, though there be events which cannot be fitted in to point to other events of divine or human working, yet they are not narrated without a purpose? Who would not like to refer them to some spiritual sense, if he could, or allow that they should be so referred by anyone who can? (xvii, 3; *cf.* xv, 27).

There is many a grand utterance on the lips of Jewish historian and prophet which altogether transcends the immediate occasion which called it forth, and has its entire fulfilment only in Christ and his Church, the immediate event of the hour being a type of the greater to come. Such are the Canticle of Anna, 1 Kings (Sam.) ii, so explained in c. 4; the promises of God to David about his son, very imperfectly fulfilled in Solomon (2 Kings [Sam.] vii 12-16; Ps. lxxxviii), as shown in cc. 8, 9, 13; also the contents of sundry other psalms, clearly Messianic (cc. 11, 12, 16-19). Of the authorship of the Psalms St Augustine says: "Their opinion seems to me more credible, who assign all those one hundred and fifty psalms to his (David's) work" (c. 14). On the Messianic interpretation of a psalm he remarks shrewdly: "Any such alleged testimony ought to be supported by the context of the entire psalm; or if not everything supports, at least nothing should go against it; therefore the whole psalm has to be explained." Otherwise, he says, we are like those people who make *centos* of verses read backwards-way (*retrogrado carmine*), getting their own meaning out of a poem made for quite another purpose (xvii, 15).

The Song of Solomon, allegorical throughout, is dismissed in these few words: "The Canticle of Canticles is a spiritual delight of holy souls in the nuptial union of the King and Queen of the City, that is Christ and his Church. But this delight is wrapped up in veils of allegory, that it may be more ardently desired, and more agreeably exposed, and the Spouse may appear" (xvii, 20).

Tacite multa transimus, cura hujus operis terminandi (*ibid.*).

BOOK XVIII

THE first twenty-six chapters of this Book are a conspectus of Greek, Roman, and Assyrian history, contemporary with Jewish history from Abraham to the Babylonian Captivity. This by way of tracing the fortunes of that other City, which is not the City of God—not but that among these heathen nations there may have been found, not indeed any chosen people of God, but individual elect souls, such as Job, belonging to the spiritual Jerusalem.

To none must we suppose this to have been granted except to such as had revealed to them of God the *one Mediator of God and men, the man Christ Jesus* (1 Tim. ii 5), whose future coming in the flesh was announced to those ancient saints, as his past coming is announced to us, that by him one and the same faith should carry through to God, unto the City of God, the House of God, the Temple of God, all the predestinate (xviii, 47).

This survey of profane history is not felicitous. Materials were wanting. It is hard making bricks without straw (Exod. v 10-18).

I quote the story of the origin of the Septuagint as Augustine tells it, because its further application throws light on Augustine's habit of mind as a commentator.

Ptolemy Philadelphus, King of Egypt, had heard the Scriptures spoken of as divine, and desired to have them in his fine library at Alexandria. Accordingly he asked Eleazar, then High Priest, for a copy. The priest sent them in Hebrew; then the King asked for translators. Seventy-two were given him, six from each tribe, accomplished Hebrew and Greek scholars; hence the custom of calling their production the Septuagint. Now tradition certainly has it (*traditur sane*) that so wonderful, stupendous, and altogether divine was the agreement in their words, that though they sat each apart to do their work—for so Ptolemy had thought fit to test their accuracy—in no one synonym, nor in the order of the words, was there any discrepancy between one version and another, but as though there had been one translator only, their versions were all one, because of a truth there was one Spirit in all (xviii, 42).

St Jerome's translation from the Hebrew had just appeared, and created a stir by being in many places at variance with the Septuagint, which, or translations from which, had hitherto been read in the churches. Whereupon St Augustine remarks:

Even though one Spirit, indubitably divine, had not appeared [in the 72], but in usual human fashion they had compared their several versions, and so agreed upon a common text, even so no one translator [not even Jerome] ought to be preferred to them; but now that such a sign of divine sanction has appeared in them, clearly any veracious translator from the Hebrew into any other language either agrees with the Septuagint, or if he does not agree, we must believe there is some prophetic depth of mystery (*altitudo prophetica*) latent there (c. 43).

There are passages in the Hebrew, not found in the Septuagint, marked with asterisks in St Augustine's day, and others, marked with hooks, in the Septuagint, but not in the Hebrew. In St Augustine's judgement, the same Holy Spirit who preferred to say some things through Jeremiah, others through Isaiah, chose sometimes to speak through the Hebrew alone, sometimes by the Septuagint alone: thus he holds the inspiration of both sets of passages. But when the Hebrew and Septuagint are at variance with one another, there comes in *altitudo prophetica*. Thus, where we read with the Hebrew: *Yet forty days, and Niniveh* (Jonas iii 4), the Septuagint has, *Yet three days*. St Augustine says: " If I am asked, which of these Jonas said, I think rather what is read in the Hebrew, *Yet forty days*." So much for the literal sense. But he argues that the Seventy were inspired to depart from the literal and substitute a mystical number.

It was a narrative of an event in the history of the city of Niniveh, but also a mystical narrative, signifying something beyond the measure of that city; just as the prophet Jonas himself being in the whale's belly for three days made an historical event, yet an event further significant of him who is Lord of all prophets being in the depth of hell for three days (Matt. xii 40). Wherefore if by that city we may rightly understand the Church of the Gentiles in prophetic figure, which was subverted—*i.e.*, converted by repentance, so as to be no longer what it had been; and this conversion was the work of Christ, taking, as we may reckon it, either forty days or three days—we have here a figure of Christ; and the forty days are the days he spent with his disciples after his resurrection, or again three days, because he rose again on the third day; so you find the one number (40) in his Ascension, the other (3) in his Resurrection (xviii, 44).

But in Book XV, treating of the numbers assigned in the Septuagint, higher than the Hebrew, for the ages of the patriarchs (Gen. v-xi), St Augustine sees no mystery, but conjectures the discrepancy to have arisen from the unfortunate industry of the copyist who wrote out the archetype manuscript on which the labour of the Seventy depended. This man, wishing to make patriarchal longevity more credible, took it that the unit of time, called a year in the reckoning of the ages of the patriarchs, was but a tenth of our year; then, finding that at that rate some of the patriarchs became fathers before it was physically possible, he tampered with the numbers and made a botch of the whole reckoning (xv, 13-15).

St Augustine's account of the forty and the three days, the literal and mystical number allowed for Nineveh, sins against the canon of modern hermeneutics, that the mystical meaning must ever be founded upon the literal.

A Catholic will ever pay high respect to the Septuagint for the use made of it by the Apostles, and by the early Church, as also by the Oriental Church of all ages. But few would contend now for a new inspiration vouchsafed to those seventy-two Jewish translators, and still fewer for the story of their miraculous harmony, which is ridiculed by St Jerome (*Prolog. ad Pentateuch.*). St Augustine was at more pains than he need have been to conciliate the Septuagint with the Hebrew. Nor must it be assumed that the Hebrew, as we know it, is always the more correct and authentic of the two.

St Augustine defines a heretic: " They are heretics who in the Church of God entertain some unwholesome and perverse opinion, and on being rebuked refuse to alter it and square it to sound and right doctrine, but are contumacious in their resistance, refuse to amend their pestilential and deadly creed, and persist in defending the same " (c. 51). A " material " heretic is merely a man in error. We have here defined a " formal " heretic, for such alone are contumacious. This distinction of " material " and " formal " was not so clear in Augustine's day as it has become in our own. Augustine characteristically consoles himself with the reflection that heresies cannot diminish the fixed number of the elect. Would he perchance allow that, on account of heresies, that number has been fixed lower than it otherwise would have been? I think not.

BOOK XIX

THE remaining four Books treat of the end which the Two Cities severally have in view, first, of the end aimed at, which in each case is happiness, then of the Judgement that shall overtake each, and their several allotments to Heaven and Hell. The end of the earthly City is happiness in this world, and Augustine in this book argues that happiness is not attainable here. " Who is sufficient," he asks, " with whatever flood of eloquence, to set forth in order the miseries of this life ?" (c. 4). Bodily health is uncertain; there are many ills that flesh is heir to; virtue is imperfect even in the wisest and best of us; philosophers who extol the imperturbable height of serene beatitude attainable by the wise, teach also that there are situations in which the wise man will best show his wisdom by taking his own life. " O happy life, that invokes the aid of death to bring it to an end !" (c. 4). Human society, domestic and civil, and particularly the company of friends, is an element of human happiness. Yet with what miseries is it also fraught ! Friends betray, wife and children are unfaithful, or grieve us by dying; lawsuits are incessant, wars frequent (cc. 4-7). (See above, ix, 14.)

On war he writes:

Enemies have never been wanting, nor are wanting now [to the Roman Power], in the shape of foreign nations, against whom wars always have been and are still carried on. Nay, the very extent of the Empire has engendered wars even of a more malignant type, social and civil wars . . . (c. 7). They who wage war wish for nothing else than victory; they wish by means of war to arrive at a glorious peace. For what else is victory but getting the adverse party under ? That done, there will be peace. Belligerents are not reluctant to have peace, but they want a peace to their own liking (*non ut sit pax nolunt, sed ut ea sit quam volunt*) (c. 12).

Sayings abundantly verified within our experience!

Of a judge, presiding over the judicial torture, now of slave witnesses, now of slave prisoners, St Augustine treats in this curious passage:

Judges are often compelled to search out the truth by the torture of innocent witnesses in a cause wherein they have no concern. Or again, a man is tortured in his own cause; while his guilt is matter of enquiry, he is put to agony; even though innocent, he pays a most certain penalty of an uncertain crime, not because his guilt is discovered, but because his innocence is not clear. Thus often the judge's ignorance is the innocent man's calamity. Still more intolerable and lamentable is the case where the accused prefers to escape from this life by suicide rather than bear his torments any longer, and thereby seems to say that he has committed a crime which really he has not committed.[1] The judge has tortured this innocent man to gain knowledge, and caused his death in lack of knowledge. In these blind dealings of social life shall the wise man take his seat on the judge's bench or not take it? Certainly he will take his seat, obliged thereto by a duty to human society which he considers it wrong to abandon. He holds it for no sin on his part that innocent men are tortured in other men's causes; that the accused generally are overcome by stress of pain to making false confessions of guilt, and so are punished in their innocence, having been already tortured in their innocence; that though not punished with death, they frequently die under torture or of its effects; that sometimes also the accusers, whose motive was to benefit human society, are punished by the judge in ignorance for being unable to prove their charges, though the charges were true, where the witnesses lie, and the accused holds out extraordinarily against torture and refuses to confess. All this long chain of evils, the judge sets down for no sins of his, for, like a wise man, he does things with no will to do harm, but under constraint of ignorance, and at the same time under constraint of sitting in judgement, human society compelling him thereto (c. 6).

[1] The Augustinian Latin here is lengthier, and elaborately rhetorical.

Not the iniquity of the judge, but certainly the iniquity of the system, to put a man to pain and torment before any guilty act is proved against him! A great stain this was on the jurisprudence of our ancestors, witness the imprisonments in that English Bastille, the Tower of London, in the sixteenth century.

Augustine concludes:

> Let him avow his misery, whoever considers in sorrow these evils, so great, so dreadful, so cruel. As for the man [the Stoic] who either suffers or reflects upon them without grief of soul, he is much more miserable in fancying himself happy because he has lost all human feeling (c. 7).

Augustine certainly shows that the goods of this life are uncertain, and traversed with innumerable evils. But he does not show that they are not good things while they last. As for the evils of to-morrow, *to-morrow will take care of itself* (Matt. vi 34). Of course, there is no stable, full, and unmixed happiness here below. If such stability and fullness be brought into the definition of happiness, the Augustinian position holds. But the more common estimate holds that happiness, like virtue, beauty, free will, admits of degrees, and may be said to exist even where it is not perfect. (See above, ix, 14; xix, 4.)

In his *Enarrationes in Psalmos, enarr. 2 in ps.* 36, St Augustine owns that, taking life as a whole, our brighter hours are more numerous than our sad ones. He says: "Our intervals of gladness are certainly more numerous and more protracted than our times of hardship (*laeta plura et longiora sunt certe quam dura*), and those hard times are shorter and fewer, to the end that we may be able to go through them." In an average life, how much more numerous are the hours of health than sickness! It would be a bad railway on which there was an accident every quarter of a mile.

It is, however, St Augustine's habit to depreciate the temporal and natural in comparison with the supernatural and eternal. So he depreciates temporal happiness by comparison.

Here we are called happy when we have peace, such little peace as can be had in a good life; but that happiness, in comparison with our final happiness, proves to be altogether misery (c. 10).

And this is the explanation of his depreciation of mere natural virtue—that feature of Augustinianism which was so exaggerated by the Jansenists. The depreciation is comparative, not absolute. In this very chapter (xix, 10) he speaks of natural virtue as the right use of the goods and evils of life. But then he adds it is " true virtue "—*i.e.*, supernatural, when one refers all things to " that peace, so excellent, so great, that there can be nothing better or greater."

We cannot pass over St Augustine's celebrated definition of peace.

Peace of the body is the well-ordered apportionment of its components. Peace of the irrational soul is the well-ordered rest of appetite. Peace of the rational soul is the well-ordered agreement of cognition and conduct. Peace of body and soul is the well-ordered life and good estate of animal existence. Peace of mortal man with God is well-ordered obedience in faith under the eternal law [*cf. Faust.*, xxii, *cf.* 27]. The peace of mankind is a well-ordered concord. The peace of a household is a well-ordered concord of the members of the community in the matter of command and obedience. The peace of a city is the well-ordered concord of the citizens in the matter of command and obedience.[1] The peace of the Heavenly City is social life in thorough good order and concord for the enjoyment of God and of one another's company in God. The peace of all things is the tranquillity of order. Order is an arrangement of components equal and unequal, assigning the proper place to each (c. 13).

He says against the Manichees, and by implication against the Jansenists:

[1] It strikes us in these democratic days that this is rather the peace of an army than of a city. We should look for some mention of agreement among classes.

There cannot be a nature in which there is no good. Not even the devil's nature is an evil thing inasmuch as it is a nature, but perversity makes it evil. God does not take away all that he has given to nature, but he takes something away and leaves something.

The following might serve as an introduction to St Ignatius' *Spiritual Exercises:*

God, wise creator and just ordainer of the natures of all things that be, having set up the mortal race of mankind as the greatest ornament of his material creation, has given to men certain goods proper to this life—to wit, temporal peace according to the small measure of mortal life, consisting of the preservation and well-being and mutual fellowship of man's race, and in all that is necessary for the maintenance or recovery of this peace, such as fit and proper objects of sense, this visible light, good air to breathe, wholesome water to drink, and all that makes for the nourishing, covering, curing, and adorning of the body—under this most equitable bargain, that any mortal who makes a right use of these goods adapted to the use of mortals, shall receive ampler and better goods—namely, the peace of immortality, and the glory and honour proper thereto in life everlasting, to enjoy God and his neighbour in God; but he who makes a wrong use shall not receive the one and shall lose the other.

This is St Augustine's reply to the Academics, the sceptics of his day, who held that all things are uncertain.

The City of God absolutely detests such doubt as madness. We do comprehend many things by thought and reason, and have most certain knowledge of them, albeit such knowledge is small on account of the *corruptible body weighing down the soul* (Wisd. ix 15), since, as the Apostle says, *we know in part* (1 Cor. xiii 9). That City believes the senses which the soul uses through the body, in evidence of each object of sense. Whoever thinks the senses are never to be believed, is all the more miserably deceived for his caution. Our City believes also the Holy Scriptures, which we call Canonical, both Old and New, whence that faith is conceived whereby the *just man lives* (Heb. ii 4), whereby we believe without doubting so long as we *wander as pilgrims away from the Lord* (2 Cor. v 6). So long as this faith is kept safe and sure, we may continue without just reprehension to have our doubts of things that we have not perceived either by sense or reason, things that have not been notified to us by canonical Scripture, things again that have not come to our knowledge through witnesses of unimpeachable credit.

The leisure (*otium*, σχολή) of a student—not a student working for an examination, but one who enjoys learned leisure—is set over against the activity of business or political life. "The leisure of a student should not exclude all thought of the profit of his neighbour; nor the activity of a business man fail to seek after the contemplation of God. In leisure a man ought not to revel in the luxury of having nothing to do; he should be occupied with either the investigation or the discovery of truth; one should advance in truth, hold fast what one finds, and not grudge communicating it to another. The thing to love in an active life is not honour or power, for *all things are vanity under the sun* (Eccles. i 14), but the work itself." There follows the famous sentence: "Let him understand that he is no bishop, who loves to rule and not to be useful to his flock" (*intelligat se non esse episcopum, qui praeesse dilexerit, non prodesse*, xix, 19).

Chapter 21 of this Book carries us back to ii, 21, where we have an analysis of Cicero's treatise *De Republica*, evidently extant in St Augustine's time, but now existing only in fragments. Cicero there defines *respublica* as *res populi*, the "property, or interest of the people." And he defines the "people" as "a gathering of a multitude, associated by consent as to law and right (*juris consensu*) and community of interest." But there is no law and right where there is no justice (*non est jus, ubi justitia nulla est*). And justice is the virtue that distributes to every one his own. But, says Augustine, where God does not come in for his own, but divine honours are paid to impure demons, as was the case in ancient Rome, then surely there is no justice, therefore no people, and no republic. "True justice is only in that republic whose founder and ruler

6

is Christ." All this is said in the second book, and reasserted here. However, in c. 24, he relents from this paradox, and, defining a people as "a gathering of a rational multitude, associated in harmonious common possession of the things that it loves," he allows the old *populus Romanus* to have been a people, and the *respublica* of Cicero's day a true republic.

Pius V condemned the saying of Michael le Bay (Baius): "The virtues of philosophers are vices." Yet Augustine had written:

> As for the virtues which it (the mind ignorant of the true God) seems to have, whereby it commands the body . . . such virtues, unless they are referred to God, are rather vices than virtues. Though some reckon them true moral virtues, when they are practised for their own sake, and not referred to any further end, even then they are inflated with pride, and therefore they are to be judged not virtues, but vices (xix, 25).

We have offered some explanation of this language already (xix, 10). Still we may regret it, and hold it for injudicious. For an act, let us say, of kindness to be naturally good, it is not necessary to refer it to God explicitly: enough that we do not bend it away from God by any perverse motive—*e.g.*, of ostentation. Nor can we assume that every such act in a pagan was done out of ostentation, or "inflated with pride," or that pagans never looked to God as *a rewarder to them that seek after him* (Heb. xi 6). He admits in this very Book that pagans such as Varro (c. 22) and Porphyry (c. 23) had some knowledge of the one true God, as St Paul told the Athenians that they might well have (Acts xvii 27-28; Rom. i 19). But to Augustine the pagan world was one hideous mass of corruption, *massa damnata*, by reason of original sin, on which matter he never sufficiently distinguishes between the *supernatural* which that sin lost, and the *natural* which it did not take away. He often speaks as though he saw in paganism no soundness of any-kind, no light from heaven vouchsafed anywhere. Clement of Alexandria, on the other hand, says that as God sent prophets to the Jews, so he sent the pagan world philosophers. The Church has condemned these propositions of Quesnel: " The will that is not prevented by grace has no light except to go astray, no ardour except to cast itself headlong, no strength except to wound itself; it is capable of all evil, and incapable of any good." " Without grace, we can love nothing but to our own condemnation." " All knowledge of God . . . in heathen philosophers, without grace, produces nothing but presumption, vanity, and opposition to God " (propp. 39, 40, 41, in Bull *Unigenitus*). What Augustine said of St John Chrysostom, that had he foreseen the Pelagian heresy he would have been more guarded in his language,[1] has been well applied to his own writings, considering the purposes to which Calvinists and Jansenists have wrested them. My own mind is intimately convinced that the pagan world has found in God a more merciful and considerate judge than it would have had in his great servant, Augustine of Hippo.

[1] *Vobis nondum litigantibus securius loquebatur*, "he was less careful what he said before your contention started " (*Cont. Julian*, i, 22).

BOOK XX

THIS Book deals with the Scripture prophecies of the Last Judgement.

God is always judging, but in the distribution of temporal blessings his judgements are unsearchable, and will appear unmistakably only at the Last Day.

We know not by what judgement of God it is that this good man is poor, and that evil man rich; this man in joy, who for his profligate character we think ought to have been tormented with griefs; that other in sorrow, whose laudable life persuades us that he ought to have been in joy; the innocent party goes out of court, not merely uncompensated, but actually condemned; the wicked is in excellent health, the pious is wasting away with illness; robust young men rob on the high ways, while they who could not have found it in their hearts to utter a harsh word are afflicted with a variety of terrible diseases; children useful to society are carried off by an untimely death, while others, who one would think should never have been born, live long years; a man laden with crimes is raised to posts of honour, another of irreproachable character is buried in the darkness of obscurity. Who can enumerate the cases of this sort? It would be something if even the very anomaly, so to say, were constant; if, in this life, only the wicked gained these transitory and earthly goods, and only the good suffered the like evils, this might be ascribed to the just, or even the gracious judgement of God, that they who were not destined to gain the everlasting good things that make their possessors happy, should have temporal goods, whether to beguile them in their malice, or to comfort them in God's mercy; while such as were not destined to suffer everlasting torment should be afflicted with temporal evils, whether in expiation of their sins whatsoever and howsoever small, or by way of exercise to make full their virtues. But now that not only the good are ill-off, and the evil well-off, which looks like injustice, but also often ill luck attends the evil and good luck the good, the judgements of God are so much the more unsearchable. Anyhow we learn not to make much account of either good or evil things that we see befalling good and bad people in common. . . . Though the just judgements of God, so many and nearly all of them, are hidden from the perceptions and understandings of mortals, this at least is not hidden from the faith of the pious, that that is just which is hidden (c. 2).

In c. 5 St Augustine refers us to a long letter on the End of the World, which he wrote to Hesychius, Bishop of Salona, now numbered among his Epistles, No. 199. He deals there with Daniel's weeks, with blended prophecies of the fall of Jerusalem and the end of the world, one being a type and forerunner of the other; and thus he finally concludes:

Wherefore he who fixes an earlier date for the Lord's coming announces the more desirable alternative, but is the more thrown out if he is wrong. I hope it may be true, because it will be matter of regret if it is not true. But he who assigns a later date to the Lord's coming, and still believes in, hopes for, and loves his coming, certainly, if he is deceived, is the more happily deceived. He will have the greater patience, if it shall be as he says; the greater joy, if it shall not be. And thus, among those who love the manifestation of the Lord, the one prophet is heard with the greater pleasure, the other is believed with the greater security. But he who owns that he does not know which of these predictions is true, wishes for the one alternative, endures the other, and is wrong on neither, because neither of them does he affirm or deny. I beg you not to despise me for being such a one, because I love you for asserting what I desire to be true; and the more I love what you promise, the more reluctant I am for you to prove wrong.

The above was written just fifteen centuries ago.

Regarding the millennium (Apoc. xx 4) St Augustine writes:

This opinion [of a temporal reign of Christ on earth] would be in some sort tolerable, if spiritual delights were believed to accrue to the saints in that sabbath through the presence of Christ. We ourselves followed that opinion once. But when people tell us that they who shall have then risen are to spend their time in gluttonous carnal banquets, keeping no moderation, but going beyond all bounds of belief [read *credulitatis*] in the amount of food and drink that they consume, such fables can be believed only by carnal men.

St Augustine, leading the way in which Catholic commentators generally follow, considers the *thousand years* of Apoc. xx 1-7 to signify in mystic number the duration of the Church on earth from the Ascension till the Second Coming. During these years *Satan is bound* by the development of the strength of Christian teaching and sacraments. The saints, as they die, go—that is, their souls go—to reign with Christ in heaven till the General Resurrection. By *the rest of the dead* (ver. 5) he understands the reprobate who never arrive to life everlasting. The *until* of that verse is like the *until* of Matt. i 25; this reference, however, is not in Augustine (cc. 7, 8, 9).

On Apoc. xx 4 St Augustine insists:

We must not suppose that the souls of the pious dead are separated from the Church, which is even now the kingdom of Christ. Otherwise no *memento* would be made of them at God's altar in the Communion of the Body of Christ; nor would it profit them anything, in cases of danger of death, to have hasty recourse to Baptism, so as not to end their days unbaptised; or to the [Sacrament of] Reconciliation, if perchance they are separated from the Body of the Church, either [visibly] by being enrolled among the Penitents, or [invisibly] by their own evil conscience.[1] Why all this, except that the faithful departed are members of Christ? Their souls reign with God, though not yet reunited with their bodies, while the said thousand years are running their course.[2] There is mention only of the souls of the martyrs;

[1] The public penitents stood in the Church porch, Sunday after Sunday, waiting for their absolution, which was usually given on Maundy Thursday. We have here mention of three Sacraments, Holy Eucharist, Baptism, and undoubtedly also Penance.

[2] This makes against the Oriental doctrine of the sleep of the soul, condemned by Benedict XII, A.D. 1336.

from the part we understand the whole, all the rest of the dead belonging to the Church (c. 9).

Such, then, is *the first resurrection* (ver. 5). We are in the midst of it ourselves; *cf.* John v 25, 28, where two resurrections also are distinguished, one the conversion of the world, the other the resurrection at the Last Day.

On the text, *The mystery of iniquity is already being wrought out : only till he that restraineth now, be put out of the way* (2 Thess. ii 7), Augustine bluntly writes: "I own my utter ignorance of the meaning" (*ego prorsus quid dixerit me fateor ignorare*, c. 19). He will, however, give the surmises of others. Some take the *restraining power* to be the Roman Empire, which Augustine himself thinks to be not unlikely, and *the mystery of iniquity* —*i.e.*, Antichrist—to be Nero, who is to come to life again or even is not dead, which Augustine calls a *multum mira praesumptio*. Others take the *mystery of iniquity* to be the multiplication of bad men in the Church; and the *restraining power* to be the fact that they are not yet sufficiently numerous to make a body for Antichrist to head—a difficulty, one would think, that ought to have been got over by this time.

On 1 Thess. iv 15-17, Augustine writes:

The question is asked whether those whom Christ is to find alive here on earth—whom the Apostle personates in himself and his contemporaries—are never to die at all; or whether, in the very instant in which, along with the risen saints, they shall be caught up in the clouds to meet Christ in the air, they shall pass with wonderful swiftness through death to immortality.

Conjecturally, he supports the second alternative, but very sensibly concludes:

That the resurrection of the dead is to take place in the flesh, when Christ is to come to judge the living and the dead, that we must believe, if we want to be Christians. But if we cannot perfectly comprehend how the resurrection is to take place, not on that account is *our faith vain* (c. 20; 1 Cor. xv 14)

Augustine quotes these lines of Malachy, the last of the Old Testament: *Lo I send you Elias the Thesbite, ere the day of the Lord, great and terrible, come: he will bring back the hearts of fathers to their children, and the hearts of children to their fathers, lest I come and strike the land with a curse* (Mal. iv 5, 6). On which Augustine writes: " That through this great and wonderful prophet Elias their law will be expounded to them, in the last age before the Judgement, and the Jews will come to believe in the true Christ—that is, in our Christ—such is a saying continually on the lips, and frequent in the thoughts of the faithful " (c. 29). (*Cf.* Rom. xi 25-32.) And then the end, and not till then.

And in his name the Gentiles shall hope (Isa. xlii 4).

Who could have expected the Gentiles to hope in Christ, when he was held fast, bound, smitten, mocked, crucified? when his very disciples had lost the hope they had begun to have in him? What was then the hope of scarcely one thief on a cross, is now the hope of nations spread far and wide. To escape everlasting death, they sign themselves with the sign of that very cross on which he died. None therefore either denies or doubts that the Last Judgement will be fulfilled through Jesus Christ in such fashion as is foretold in Holy Writ—none, I say, except him who with incredible animosity or blindness does not believe a history which has already shown its truth all the world over. In that Judgement, therefore, or round about that Judgement, we have learnt that these events are to occur, the appearance of Elias the Thesbite, the reception of the faith by the Jews, the persecution of Antichrist, the judgement of Christ, the resurrection of the dead, the separation of humankind good and evil, the conflagration of the world and renovation of the same. We must believe that all these events will come, but in what ways and in what order they will come, experience will teach better than the present intelligence of man can exactly conceive. I think, however, that they will come in the order in which they have been mentioned by me.

BOOK XXI

THIS Book treats of everlasting punishment, the end of the City of Evil, Babylon.

The writer is confronted with the difficulty, how can a body burn for ever without being consumed, or suffer pain for ever without dying? He answers that there are many things in nature, of which we cannot tell how they can be, and yet they evidently are. St Augustine had an eye for curiosities: of this we get many glimpses in his writings. In cc. 4-8 he gives a list of natural wonders, as they appeared to men of his time; some of them modern science would recognise and explain, some it would pronounce fabulous. I have relegated them to an Appendix.

In xxi, 12, St Augustine gives us a compendium of that much controverted work, *Of Reprehension and Grace*, which he was engaged on at the time (*A.*, iv, 426):

The reason why everlasting punishment appears hard and unjust to human ideas is because in this infirmity of our mortal state we have no adequate grasp of that exceeding high and pure wisdom which would enable us to form an idea of the enormity of man's first transgression. The higher man's enjoyment of God, the greater his impiety in forsaking God: destroying in himself a good gift that might have lasted for ever, he became deserving of evil to last for ever. Hence is the whole clay of humanity a condemned clay [*massa damnata* (*cf.* Rom. ix 21; v, 18)], because the original perpetrator of this crime, together with the race that had its root in him, is punished with a just and due punishment, such as no man is delivered from otherwise than by mercy and undue grace. Thus is the human race divided into two divisions [the Two Cities]. In the one is shown the power of merciful grace, in the other that of just vengeance. Both aspects of the dispensation cannot be shown in all men. If all remained under the penalties of a just condemnation, in none could appear the merciful grace of the Redeemer. Again, if all were translated from darkness to light, in none could appear the severity of the Avenger. Under that severity of vengeance come many more than under merciful grace, thereby to show what was due to all. If vengeance were rendered to all, none could justly blame the vengeance of the Avenger. Now that so many are delivered therefrom, there is ground for rendering the greatest thanks to the bounty of the Liberator.

This characteristically Augustinian sentence must not be mistaken for a dogmatic utterance of the Catholic Church. Anyone with an insight into its meaning will see that the argument is profoundly modified by a pronouncement attributed to Innocent III, and certainly now the common opinion of Catholic theologians: "The punishment of original sin is the loss of the vision of God: the punishment of actual sin is the everlasting torment of hell."[1]

While arguing that not all punishment in the next life is merely purgatorial and temporary, St Augustine fully confesses the Catholic doctrine of Purgatory.

Not all who suffer temporal punishment after death come in for the everlasting punishment which is to be after Judgement. To some, what is not remitted in this world is remitted in the world to come (xxi, 13, and further to the same effect, c. 24, *n.* 2).

In *C. D.*, xxi, cc. 17-27, St Augustine gives an interesting list of various exceptions that, as early as his time, had been taken to the universality of everlasting punishment for all who die in deadly sin. He mentions six such exceptions:

(*a*) Origen's doctrine, borrowed from Plato, *Republic*, x, and elsewhere, that neither happiness nor misery shall be everlasting in the next world, but there shall be recurring

[1] The subject is too deep for this work. I have gone into the depths of it in another volume, a translation with notes of the *De correptione et gratia*.

periods of reward or punishment, followed by new probation; thus not even the devils shall be tormented everlastingly.

Statement, xxi, c. 17.

Reply, c. 23.

(*b*) That at the Last Day the prayers of the Saints shall be so powerful as finally to deliver every human being from everlasting punishment.

Statement, xxi, c. 18.

Reply, c. 24.

(*c*) That all who have ever received the holy Eucharist shall escape everlasting punishment.

Statement, xxi, c. 19.

Reply, c. 25.

(*d*) That all who have been baptised and made their Communion in the Catholic Church shall be finally saved.

Statement, xxi, c. 20.

Reply, c. 25.

(*e*) That all shall be finally saved who die in the Catholic faith.

Statement, xxi, c. 21.

Reply, c. 26.

(*f*) That none shall perish everlastingly who gives alms.

Statement, xxi, c. 22.

Reply, c. 27.

To take these six heads in order:

(*a*) Of Origen Augustine writes: " For this saying [that the devils shall some day be restored to the society of the holy angels], and for other of his tenets, especially that of perpetual recurring periods of happiness and misery, the Church has not undeservedly put him under her ban." Origen is in contradiction with Matt. xxv 41; Apoc. xx 9, 10. " Not to argue against God, but to obey the divine precept while still there is time, that is what they ought to do who wish to avoid everlasting punishment," says St Augustine (xxi, 23).

Origen's fantastic theory of creation, some approach to that of the Manichees, is noted in *C. D.*, xi, 23.

(*b*) St Augustine writes:

> There are people, such as I myself have come across in our conferences, who say: " A merciful God will grant their pardon [pardon of all sinful mankind] to the prayers and intercessions of his Saints; we cannot suppose that, in the fulness and perfection of their sanctity, the Saints will lose their hearts of mercy; or that they who formerly prayed for their enemies, when they were themselves not without sin, will not pray for their suppliants at the last day, when themselves they shall have entered into a sinless state " (c. 18).

They argue from such texts as these: *Shall God forget to show mercy? or shall he hold back his mercies in his anger?* (Ps. lxxvi 10). And again: *God hath shut up all in unbelief, in order to have mercy on all* (Rom. xi 32). They appeal to Jonah's threat against Nineveh, which was never carried out; and thence conclude that the sentence of everlasting punishment, though threatened in all justice, will yet be revoked in mercy. Augustine well replies: " Certainly, all this will be as they say, if not God's words but human surmises shall have the more weight " (c. 23). To the psalm he says that in this life God will not hold back his mercies from the *vessels of mercy* (Rom. ix 23), whom he intends to save. Further, he mentions an opinion that God has mercy even upon the vessels of his wrath, in that they suffer milder and lighter penalties than they deserve: on which opinion Augustine remarks, " I am not to be supposed to affirm this view merely because I do not oppose it " (c. 24).

Niniveh, he contends, really was overthrown, as Jonah foretold, inasmuch as its wickedness was overthrown—not a satisfactory explanation, because that was not what Jonah meant to foretell.

On Romans xi 32, the writer of the treatise *De correptione et gratia* comments characteristically: " Yes, he has mercy on all the vessels of mercy, both on those of the

Gentiles and those of the Jews, whom he has *predestined, called, justified, glorified* (Rom. viii 29, 30); of all that number, but not of all mankind, his purpose is to damn none" (c. 24).

(*c*) To the text alleged, *He that eateth this bread shall live for ever* (John vi 58), St Augustine appends another text, *They that do such things* as enumerated (1 Cor. vi 9, 10), things which communicants unfortunately often have done, *shall not possess the kingdom of God.* The Eucharist being the sacrament of peace and unity, he is to be said to eat the Body of Christ, and drink the Blood of Christ, *truly*, that is to his soul's salvation, who remains in the mystical Body of Christ, and does not fall away from thence by heresy or apostasy. But what of evil-living Catholics?

(*d*) The text, 1 Cor. vi 9, 10, applies to them. Only *he that persevereth to the end shall be saved* (Matt. x 22). "They do not *abide in Christ* (John vi 56) who are no members of his. And they are no members of his who make themselves *members of a harlot* (1 Cor. vi 15), unless by penance they cease to be that evil thing, and by reconciliation [sacramental absolution, see above, xxi, 9] return to this good thing" (c. 25).

(*e*) The idea of no man being lost who dies a Catholic is a misapprehension of 1 Cor. iii 11-16, as though a man founded on Christ by keeping the Catholic faith even to the end could not possibly perish everlastingly. St Augustine argues that a man in mortal sin, who has preferred the gratification of his own lust to Christ, cannot be said to be *founded on Christ.* The *fire* of 1 Cor. iii 15 he takes to be, not that of hell, but of temporal tribulation, whether in this world or the next.

(*f*) For almsgivers, appeal is made to Matt. xxv 34-46. St Augustine asks how large the alms are to be, to balance the sins committed. He quotes the text: *Do ye works worthy of penance* (Matt. iii 8) which supposes a cessation from sin; and again: *Have mercy on thine own soul, pleasing*

God (Ecclus. xxx 14); and, *He who is evil to himself, to whom shall he be good?* (*ibid.*, xiv 5). Alms, he says, as we all say, avail to pardon of past sins, not to impunity of sinning in the future.

Speaking of prayers for the dead, which avail only for those who have died in venial and not in mortal sin, St Augustine avows himself at a loss to distinguish between the two.

> Where to draw the line, and what the sins are which, while they impede entrance into the kingdom of God, nevertheless may deserve pardon through the merits of holy friends, it is very difficult to discover, very dangerous to define. I certainly, up to this time, though I have busied myself to trace the distinction out, have been unable to reach a conclusion. And perhaps it escapes our research, lest our zeal should flag in endeavouring to do things better and avoid all sin (xxi, 27).

The study of moral theology—also the practice of frequent confession—has carried later generations further on this ground.

BOOK XXII

This Book is on the consummation of the Heavenly City in the resurrection of the just.

In c. 1 there is a happy phrase descriptive of man in the state of grace, " an earthly animal, to be sure, but worthy of heaven " (*terrenum quidem animal, sed coelo dignum*).

In the same, St Augustine makes a valuable admission, that the number of the elect is not necessarily limited by the number of angels who fell—" thence to supply and restore the moiety of angels who fell, that thus that well-beloved City in heaven may not be deprived of its due number of citizens, nay, possibly may rejoice in their augmentation."

St Augustine argues the credibility of Christ's Resurrection and Ascension from the fact that it has come to be so widely believed, and that on the evidence of simple, unsophisticated witnesses.

If the thing believed is incredible, it is also incredible that the incredible should have been so believed. Here we have three incredible things, which nevertheless have come about. It is incredible that Christ should have risen in the flesh, and with that flesh ascended into heaven; it is incredible that the world should have believed a thing so incredible; it is incredible that men, destitute of nobility and rank, numbers and skill, should have been able so effectively to persuade the world, and even the learned men in it. Of these three incredibles, our opponents refuse to believe the first; the second they are forced to believe; and how that second came about they cannot say unless they believe the third.

Of the martyrs he says happily: " They were bound, imprisoned, scourged, racked, burnt, rent, butchered—and they multiplied " (*ligabantur*, *includebantur*, *caedebantur*, *torquebantur*, *urebantur*, *laniabantur*, *trucidabantur*, *et multiplicabantur*, c. 6). Augustine is ever the rhetorician of his age.

In c. 8, not the least interesting of the whole work, Augustine gives a list of miracles happening under his own inspection. I have translated the whole as Appendix B.

In c. 9 he says that these miracles may be wrought immediately by God himself, or by the ministry of the souls of the martyrs, or by that of the angels, but they all attest the faith in which the resurrection of the body is preached.

In c. 10 he repeats what he had said before (viii, 27).

> We do not build temples to our Martyrs as though they were gods, but memorials, or shrines (*memorias*), as to dead men whose spirits live with God. Nor do we there set up altars, to sacrifice to the Martyrs, but to God alone, God of the Martyrs and our God. In this sacrifice all the men of God, who in confession of their allegiance to him have overcome the world, are named in due place and order, but are not invoked by the sacrificing priest.[1] The reason is, because he is sacrificing to God, not to them, because he is God's priest, not theirs, although it is in their Memorial Shrine that he sacrifices. The sacrifice itself is the Body of Christ, which is not offered to them, because it is what they themselves are (xxii, 10).

The last phrase has its explanation in St Paul. *We, being many, are one bread, one body* (1 Cor. x 17); and in St John Chrysostom, writing on that text: " We are that very Body itself. For what is the Bread? The Body of Christ. And what do they become who partake thereof? The Body of Christ " (Hom. 24 in 1 Cor.).

It is St Augustine's opinion that " in the resurrection, everyone will receive that bodily stature which he had in his prime, even though he has died an old man; or would

[1] There is no direct invocation of the Saints in the Mass to this day. The nearest approach is in the *Confiteor*, the prayer before the *Orate fratres*, and some of the Collects.

have had, if he has died before that age" (c. 15). But, he adds, "if any one will have it that each human being shall rise again in that bodily stature which he had when he died, we should not go out of our way to contradict him" (c. 16). "Some say that women shall not rise again in the female sex, but all in the male; but they seem to me wiser who have no hesitation in affirming that all shall rise again in their own sex" (c. 17). St Augustine assumes that whatever has been part of a human body (*quod naturaliter inerat corpori*), down to the very hair and nails, will rise again in that body, not necessarily as the same tissue, but somewhere in the body, so disposed as to avoid deformity (c. 19). This opinion, however, outruns faith, and is not taken nowadays. Palmieri (*De novissimis*, p. 130), writes: "Since the bodies of living animals are in continual flux, and undergoing gradual change perpetually, it is not requisite that at the resurrection the whole matter should be resumed by the soul that was ever united to it during the whole course of its mortal life; for at that rate the bodies would be swollen to a huge and enormous size." On this matter of the resurrection, on which we have no experience, we must leave much to the wisdom and power of God; and subtle speculations are unprofitable.

There follow two chapters (cc. 22-23) on the miseries of human life, which we have discussed already (ix, 14-15), and one on its blessings (c. 24). They tell us nothing but what every man knows. Nor need we dwell upon the obsolete speculations of Porphyry (cc. 26-28), of whom we have seen enough already (xiii, 16). Enough to say to Porphyry and the Platonists that the risen body, in which Christians believe, is not the corruptible body, which the soul now informs, but a body which shall be no clog upon her spiritual activities.

No Father of the Church comes up to St Augustine in descanting upon the joys of heaven. They are the theme of the last two chapters of this great work.

It is possible, and very credible, that we shall have such a view of the material structure of the new heaven and the new earth as that, everywhere we turn our eyes, we shall most clearly discern God everywhere present and governing all corporeal things. God will be so known and manifest to us that we shall see him, everyone in his neighbour, see him in himself, see him in every creature, see him also by bodily vision (*per corpora*) in every corporeal thing on which the eyes of our spiritual body are directed. Our thoughts also will lie open to mutual inspection (c. 29).

How great shall be that happiness where there shall be no evil, no unappreciated good, where all shall be occupied in the praises of God! I know not what else shall be done there, where there shall be no idleness to stop activity, no want to stimulate labour. All the members and inner parts of the incorruptible body, parts which we now see distributed to meet various necessities, shall then find their free exercise in the praises of God, because then there shall be no necessity, but full, certain, secure, everlasting felicity. All the now hidden harmonies and numbers of corporeal nature, disposed within and without throughout the whole,[1] shall then be hidden no longer, and with other great and wonderful truths shall fire rational minds with delight at their rational beauty to the praise of so great an Artificer. What shall be the movements of such bodies I dare not rashly define, as I am unable to think them out. Each movement, each restful pause, each appearance that strikes the eye, shall be graceful, where nothing ungraceful shall be. Surely, wherever the spirit shall wish to be, there shall the body be at once; nor shall the spirit wish for anything that shall be unbecoming either for spirit or body. There shall be true glory, where there shall be neither mistake nor adulation in praise; there honour, denied to none that is worthy of honour, conferred on none unworthy; true peace, without opposition either from within oneself or from without. He shall be the reward of virtue, who has been the giver of virtue, and has promised himself as its reward. He shall be the end of all our desires, who shall be seen without end, loved without satiety, praised without fatigue.

Nor shall they lose their free will by the fact of their inaccessibility to the delights of sin. Their will shall be all the more free for being delivered from the delight of sin,

[1] Meaning, I suppose, the whole content and subject-matter of mathematics and music.

and given over to the delight of not sinning. By the first free will, given to man at his creation, he was able not to sin, but he was also able to sin; this last free will shall be all the more powerful inasmuch as he shall be unable to sin. But this too he shall have by the gift of God, not by the potency of his own nature.

This shall be our sabbath day, not terminated by evening; but the Lord's Day, hallowed by the resurrection of Christ, shall continue a sort of everlasting Octave, betokening eternal rest alike of spirit and body. There we shall have leisure and see; we shall see and love; we shall love and praise. Behold what shall be in the end without end. What other is our end but to arrive at a kingdom whereof there is no end?

I may say I have paid the debt of this huge work, by the help of the Lord. Let readers for whom the book is too small, or too big, pardon me. Let others for whom it is of quantity sufficient, return thanks and congratulations, not to me, but to God. Amen (xxii, 29, 30).

APPENDICES

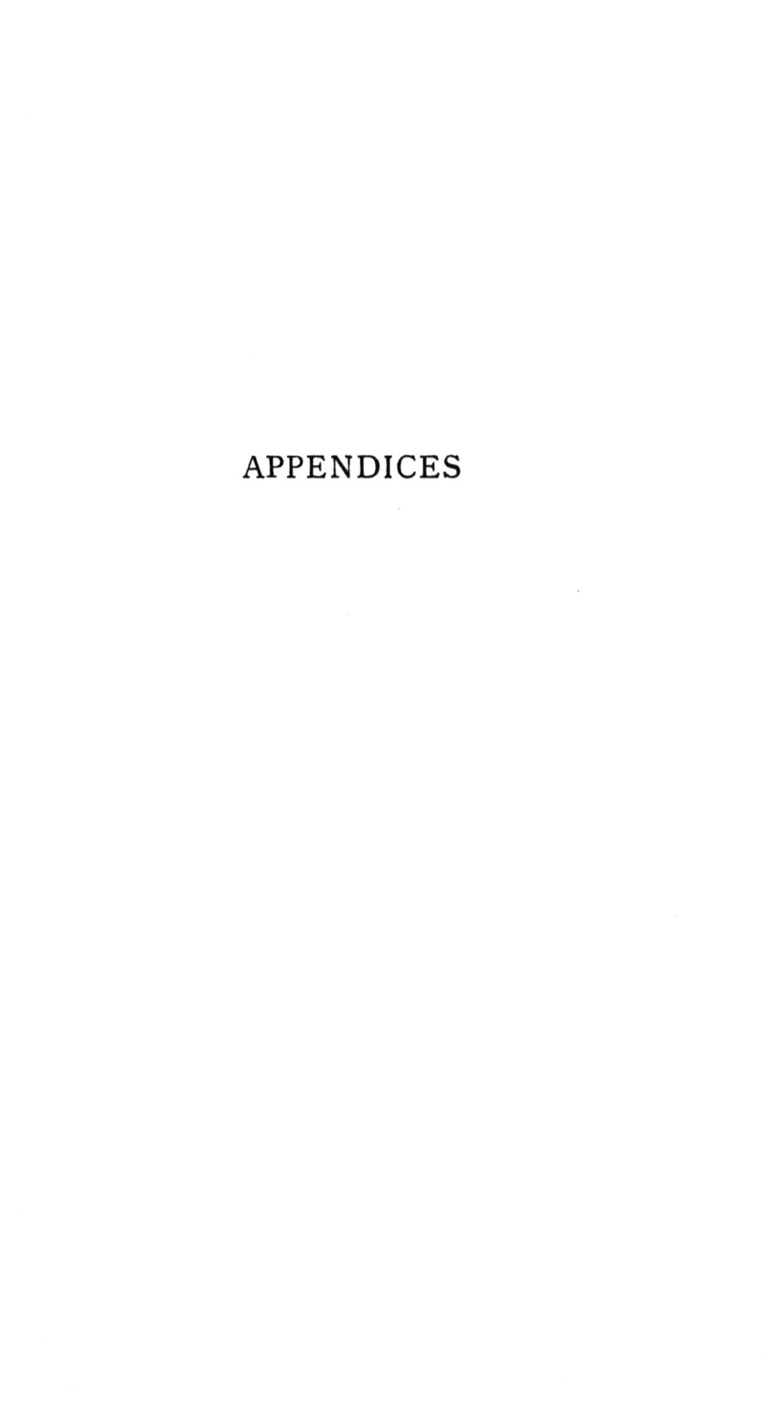

APPENDIX I

Natural Wonders, as they Appeared in St Augustine's Time

C. D. xxi, cc. 4-7.

Who but the Creator of all things has given to the flesh of a dead peacock the property of incorruption? We heard this story, and thought it incredible. Now so it happened that at Carthage this bird was served up to us cooked. We cut off what we thought a proper portion of the breast, and ordered it to be kept. After a number of days, in which any other cooked meat would have gone bad, it was brought up and presented: there was nothing about it to offend the sense of smell. It was put by again for more than thirty days with the same result; and so it remained; after a year it was a little drier and shrunken in bulk.

We know that the loadstone (*magnetem lapidem*) has a wonderful power of attracting iron. I was greatly amazed when I first saw it done. I saw an iron ring seized and hung up by the loadstone; then, as though the stone had given and communicated its power to the iron which it had seized, that same ring, being applied to another ring, hung that up, and ring stuck to ring as the first ring had stuck to the stone. There was added a third and a fourth ring, making a hanging chain of rings, not one within another, but externally adhering.

But much more wonderful is what I have heard from my brother and fellow-bishop, Severus of Milevis, about this stone. He said he was dining with Bathanarius, formerly Count of Africa, and his host brought out a loadstone, and held it under a silver plate, and put a piece of iron on the plate; then, as he moved his hand holding the loadstone underneath, the iron moved above, without the silver plate being any way affected. I have said what I have seen myself; I have said what I have heard of another, whose word I believe as I would my own eyes. I will add what

I have read of this loadstone: when a diamond is placed near it, it does not attract iron; and any iron that it may have attracted, it presently lets go as soon as the diamond comes near.

Now I do not wish all these stories to be indiscriminately believed. I do not believe them myself without any doubt at the back of my mind, except what has come under my own experience, and may readily be tested by anyone else, as the story of the lime, how it is hot in water, and cold in oil—of the loadstone, which by some insensible sucking fails to move straw, and yet attracts iron; of the peacock's flesh exempt from putrefaction, whereas putrefaction befell that of Plato; of straw so cold as not to let snow melt, so hot as to accelerate the ripening of apples. These things I know for facts, a knowledge that in some cases I share with many, in some with all. But of the narratives that I have set down, not from my own experience, but from my reading, I have not been able to find any competent witnesses to hear from them whether the stories were true, except about that fountain where lighted torches are extinguished, and torches extinguished relit (Pliny, *Natural History*, ii, 103), and about the apples of Sodom, which outside seem ripe, but within are full of soot (Tacitus, *Histories*, v). As for that fountain, I have not found anyone to tell me he had seen it in Epirus, but I knew people who had seen a similar one in Gaul, near the city of Grenoble. About the fruits on the trees of Sodom, there is not only trustworthy written history, but so many tell of their own experience that I can have no doubt on the matter. As for the other stories, my attitude is one neither of affirmation nor of denial. I have set them down because I have read them in their historians [pagans] against whom we are pleading, to show how much they believe, many of them without any reason assigned, finding it so written in their books, while they disdain believing us, when we tell them that Almighty God is likely to do what transcends their sense and experience.

There is a passage in Marcus Varro's book, *Of the Race of the Roman People*, which I will give here in his own words: " A wonderful portent appeared in the heavens; for of the well-known star of Venus, which Plautus calls Vesperugo, and Homer Hesperos, Castor writes that it assumed so portentous an appearance as to change colour, magnitude, figure, and course, a thing that never happened before, nor has happened since. The celebrated mathematicians,

Adrastus of Cyzicus and Dion of Neapolis, say that this happened in the reign of King Ogyges."[1]

Let not these unbelievers use their knowledge of natural things to obfuscate themselves, as though there could not be done in anything by divine power aught else but what they have learnt by human experience to be according to the nature of each thing. As it has not been impossible for God to set in being such natures as he willed, so it is not impossible for him to take those natures which he has set in being, and change them into whatever he wills.

APPENDIX II

A List of Miracles, coming under St Augustine's Own Notice

C. D., xxii, 8.[2]

Why, they ask, do not those miracles, which you preach of as past events, happen nowadays? I might reply that they were necessary before the world believed, to bring the world to believe; but whoever is still looking for prodigies to make him believe is himself a great prodigy for refusing to believe where the world believes. The real ground of their question is that they would not have even those old miracles believed. How, then, explain the strong faith with which Christ is everywhere sung of as having been lifted up to heaven in the flesh? How came it that, in a learned age, in an age prone to reject every impossibility, without any miracles, as you say, the world came to believe in doctrines exceeding wonderful, beyond belief? Are you, perhaps, going to say that they were believable, and therefore were believed? Why, then, do you not believe your-

[1] Ogyges, an ancient king, in whose time there was a great deluge (*C. D.*, xviii, 8). If Varro is to be believed, the planet Venus must once have been the scene of a conflagration, similar to that which astronomers of our time have observed in Nova Aurigae and other fixed stars.

[2] I have translated the whole of this chapter, which many may find the most interesting in the *City of God*.

selves? Short is our dilemma: either an incredible thing, which was not seen, was made credible by other incredible things, which, however, did take place and were seen; or else a thing so credible as not to need the support of miracles refutes their excessive incredulity, this by way of refutation of those foolish cavillers.

We cannot deny that many miracles have happened in attestation of that one great and blissful miracle whereby Christ ascended into heaven in the flesh wherein he had risen again. The miracles that were wrought, and the faith in furtherance whereof they were wrought, all are recorded in the same veracious books. The miracles were made known to establish the faith; and by the faith which they have established the miracles have come to be much better known. They are read in public assemblies to be believed, but even in public assemblies they would not be read unless they were believed. Even now miracles are wrought in his name, either through his Sacraments or through the prayers and Memorial Shrines of his Saints; but not the same clear light is thrown upon them, they have not the fame and glory of those earlier miracles. The Canons of Scripture, which had to be fixed once for all, have caused those earlier miracles to be everywhere read out and engrained in the memory of all peoples; whereas wherever these later miracles occur, they are scarcely known by the whole town or community. Often very few know of them, the rest remaining ignorant, especially in a great city; and when they are related elsewhere and to other people, they have not the recommendation of authority, so as to be believed without difficulty or hesitation, even when both narrators and hearers are faithful Christians.

Miracle I.—The miracle that took place at Milan, while we were there (A.D. 385),when the blind man had his eyes opened to the light, might easily have come to the knowledge of many, because the city is large, and the emperor was then there, and it was witnessed by a vast concourse of people, crowding to behold the bodies of the martyrs Protase and Gervase. The place of their sepulture was hidden and quite unknown, till it was revealed to Bishop Ambrose in a dream, and they were found: on which occasion that blind man cast off his former darkness and saw light.[1]

[1] See Newman, *Historical Sketches*, i, 367-374, 443-444. St Augustine further describes this miracle in his *Confessions*, ix, 7.

Miracle II.—At Carthage, who is there except a very few who knows the cure obtained by Innocent, a former advocate in the Vicar's Court? We were present at that cure, and witnessed it with our own eyes. When my brother Alypius and I, not yet clerics, but already servants of God, came from beyond the seas, Innocent, being a most godly man, as also was his whole household, gave us hospitality, and we were staying in his house. He was under treatment for fistulas; he had many and very intricate ones on the hinder and lower part of his body. The surgeons had already cut them, and were trying to do the rest of their professional treatment by means of drugs. The operation had cost him long and severe pains. But of the many cavities one had escaped the notice of the medical men, so that they did not touch what they should have opened with the knife. All the rest of the openings they had made had healed up; this alone remained, and they were working at it in vain. The delay raised his suspicions, and he much feared that he would have to be cut again, for so another surgeon, a domestic of his, had foretold. At his first operation, the surgeons had not allowed this man to be so much as a looker-on at their proceedings, and the master had turned the man in anger out of his house, and made difficulty about taking him back. Now he broke out into a passion, and said to the surgeons: "Are you going to operate again? Am I to come to what he told me, whom you would not have present?" They derided the other man's medical capacity, and with soothing words and promises tried to allay the patient's fears. Many more days passed, and all that was done was of no avail. Still his doctors stuck to their promise, that they would close that cavity with medical appliances, and not with the knife. They called in another surgeon, now an old man, and of

---

"When the incorrupt bodies of Protase and Gervase had been laid bare and dug up, and were being honourably translated to the Ambrosian Basilica, not only were persons afflicted with unclean spirits healed, the said spirits confessing their discomfiture, but also a citizen who had been many years blind, and was well known in the city, asked the cause of the tumultuous joy of the people; and when he was told, he jumped up, and begged his guide to take him to the spot. Arrived there, he secured admittance so far as to touch with his handkerchief the bier of the death of thy saints, precious in thy sight. When he did that, and applied the handkerchief to his eyes, they were at once opened."

great repute in the faculty, Ammonius (he was still alive); he looked at the place, and promised what the others had promised as the fruit of their diligence and skill. Such authority reassured the patient, and, like one already recovered, he made jokes and bantered his domestic surgeon, who had foretold another operation. To make a long story short, so many days passed by, wasted to no purpose, that the weary and confused surgeons had to avow that there was no other cure for him except by the knife. He was terrified, troubled, and turned pale with excess of fear. When he recovered himself, he bade them all be off and never come near him again. Worn out with weeping, and fast in the clutch of necessity, he had no resource but to call in a certain Alexandrian, who was then accounted a wonderful surgeon, and bid him do what in his anger he would not have those others do. When the Alexandrian came, and saw in the scars with a professional eye the labour of the other surgeons, he acted like a gentleman, and urged his patient rather to let those who had laboured so much over him, labour which he declared he regarded with admiration, enjoy the glory of completing his cure, adding at the same time that indeed, unless he were operated upon, there was no chance of saving his life. "But," he said, "it is quite out of the way of my practice to rob others of a triumph, bought with so much labour, all for the saving of the little that is left, when I see by inspection of your scars with what extraordinary skill, industry, and diligence they have worked." Thus he was brought to consider those former surgeons again, and finally he agreed that this Alexandrian was to stand by, while they opened that cavity which, by the common verdict of all, was accounted otherwise incurable. The matter was adjourned to the next day. When the doctors were gone, the exceeding great affliction of the master set up such mourning in the household that it was like the mourning over a funeral, and we had much ado to restrain it. He was visited every day by the then Bishop of Uzalis, Saturninus of holy memory, and by the priest Gelosus, and some deacons of the Church of Carthage, of whom the only one now left on earth is Aurelius, now bishop, to be named by us with all honour; we have often talked with him on this incident, and we find that he remembers it well, as we relate it. When these persons came to pay the sufferer their usual evening visit, he asked them with piteous tears, to deign to attend in the morning at what was to be his funeral rather than his pain. Such fear had come over him from the previous sufferings that he had no doubt he should die in the hands of the surgeons. They comforted him, exhorting him to put his trust in God and manfully to endure his will. Thence we fell to prayer. We knelt as usual, and bowed our heads to earth. He flung himself down as though he had been upset by a heavy push, and began to pray. But in what accents, with what earnestness, with what emotion of soul, with what a flood of tears, with what groans and sobs, shaking all his limbs and almost stopping his breath—who can detail it in words! Whether the others prayed, and were not distracted by this exhibition, I did not know. For my part I could not pray at all, and I only remember saying this briefly in my heart: "Lord, what prayers of thy servants dost thou hear, if thou dost not hear these?" (*Domine, quas tuorum preces exaudis, si has non exaudis?*) It seemed to me, there was nothing further to be added except that he should expire praying. We rose, received the bishop's blessing, and departed. He asked us to attend in the morning, we exhorted him to cheer up. The dreaded day dawned; the servants of God attended as they had promised to attend; the surgeons came in: all things are prepared as the occasion required; the awful instruments are brought out; all minds are in an agony of suspense. They who were of higher authority endeavour to raise his drooping courage with their consolations; his limbs are arranged on a couch, ready for the hands of the operator. The bandages are untied, the place laid bare, the surgeon inspects, and armed and intent he looks for that cavity to cut. He searches with his eyes, feels with his fingers, tries in short all ways; he finds—a perfectly whole scar (*firmissimam cicatricem*). What was the joy and praise and thanksgiving to the merciful and almighty God, pouring from the mouth of all with tears of joy! That is not to be committed to my words: let it be imagined rather than spoken.

Miracle III.—Also at Carthage a pious woman, named Innocentia, one of the first rank in the city, had a cancer in her breast, a thing, as the doctors say, that no medical art can cure. Accordingly, either it is cut out, according to the usual practice, and the part on which it grows is separated from the body, or else, that the man may live a little longer, yet with the certainty of death to follow later, according to what is said to be the advice of Hippocrates, all treatment is to be dropped.[1] She had heard this from a skilled physician, a great friend of the family, and had turned to God alone in prayer. She was admonished in a dream, as Easter drew near, to station herself in the place set aside for women at the baptistery, and get the first baptised woman she met to make the sign of the cross on the place (*signaret ei locum signo Christi*). She did so, and the cure followed immediately. As for the doctor, who had told her to admit no treatment, if she wished to live a little longer, when he examined her and found her quite well, though he knew by his former inspection that the disease had been there, he asked her excitedly what remedy she had used, desiring, so far as one can understand, to know what the medical appliance was that had falsified Hippocrates' axiom. When he had heard from her the true state of the case, he is said to have replied with a wit becoming a religious man: he assumed a scornful tone and look, so that she was afraid of his using disrespectful language of Christ: " I thought," he said, " you would have had something startling to tell me." And when she was all in a tremor, he said presently: " What great thing was it for Christ to cure a cancer, he who raised to life a man four days dead ?" When I heard the story, I was moved to much indignation to think that in a city, and in a person certainly not ill-known, so extraordinary a miracle should have been wrought, and nobody know of it. Whereupon I thought it my duty to admonish, and almost to scold her. She answered me that she had made no secret of the matter. Then I asked of the ladies about her, her chief friends, whether they had known the fact before. They replied that they had been in entire ignorance of it. Then I said: " This is the way that you make no secret of it, allowing your closest friends to know nothing about it." After questioning her briefly, I made her tell the whole story in detail, the others listening and greatly wondering and glorifying God.

Miracle IV.—Who knows the story of the gouty doctor in the same city ? We, however, know it, and a very few

[1] There are various emendations here. The most tempting would be to omit the *aut* before *ut aliquanto*, and put it in before *secundum Hippocratis*, and that would suit our idea of surgery, that the patient is likely to die sooner of his disease than of his doctor. But in the fifth century, I fear, death ran rather with the doctor. The manuscript reading appears to be sound in the light of what comes eight lines lower down.

brethren whom it has been able to reach. The story is this. This doctor had given in his name for baptism, and, the day before the baptism was to take place, certain black boys with long hair, whom he understood to be demons, appearing in his sleep, did their best to urge his not being baptised that year. He did not give in to them, even when they stamped on his feet, and caused him most agonising pain, such as he had never experienced before. He the rather overcame them, and made no delay in being washed in the laver of regeneration, as he had vowed. In the very moment of baptism he was not only delivered from the unusual pain which he was suffering, but was set free from the gout altogether. He lived a long time afterwards, but never more had trouble in his feet.

Miracle V.—A native of Curubis, who had been an actor, was made whole in his baptism, not only from paralysis, but also from a deformity of his privy parts; and came up from the fountain of regeneration free from both troubles, as though he had never had anything of the sort in his body. Who knows this except Curubis, and those very few persons who have anywhere had opportunity to hear the story? We, however, when it came to our knowledge, made the man come to Carthage at the bidding of the holy bishop Aurelius; though we had had the narrative before from informants of whose credit we could have no doubt.

Miracle VI.—We have in our city (Hippo) one Hesperius, a man of the rank of Colonel He has in the territory of Fussala a farm called Zubedi. Finding his house haunted with malignant spirits to the distress of his cattle and slaves, he asked our priests, in my absence, for one of them to go there, that the demons might yield to his prayers. One went and offered there the sacrifice of the Body of Christ, praying all he could for the cessation of the annoyance. By the mercy of God it ceased at once.

Miracle VII.—This Hesperius had got from a friend some holy earth, brought from Jerusalem, from the place of Christ's sepulchre. He had hung it in his bedroom, to protect himself from the infestation of the Evil One. When his house was delivered from that infestation, he bethought himself what he should do with this earth, which for reverence he did not like keeping any longer in his bedroom. It so happened that my colleague, Maximin, Bishop of the city of Synita, and myself were at hand. He asked us to come; we came; and when he had told us the whole story, he also asked us to have the earth buried somewhere where an Oratory might be established, that Christians might gather to celebrate the worship of God. We made no difficulty, and so it was done. There was there a country lad, a paralytic. When he heard of it, he begged his parents without delay to carry him to that holy place. He was brought, prayed, and at once his feet were set right, and he went away.

Miracle VIII.—There is what is called Victoria Villa, less than thirty miles from Hippo Regius. There is there a Martyrs' Memorial of the Milan martyrs, Protase and Gervase. Thither was carried a young man, and there he lay, at the point of death, looking for all the world like a corpse. What had happened to him was this. At noon, one summer's day, he was washing a horse in a pool of the river, and encountered an evil spirit. The lady of the house, according to her custom, came with her maids and some nuns to sing evensong (*vespertinos hymnos et orationes*). They began to sing their hymns. At their voices the possessed person was struck and roused from his stupor. With a horrible shriek he laid hold of the altar, and not daring or not being able to move it, he clung to it as though he had been tied or fastened there; and with loud howlings the spirit begged to be spared, acknowledging where, when, and how he had fallen on the young man. Finally he said he would go out, but threatened in going out to cut off all his limbs, naming them one after another. So saying he departed from the man. But the sufferer's eye had come down on to his cheek, hanging by a thin vein as by a root from the eye-cavity, and all the pupil, that had been black, had gone white. By this time other spectators had come in, roused by his cries, and all prostrated in prayer for him. At the sight of what had befallen him, though they rejoiced at seeing him erect and sound in mind, still they were grieved about his eye, and said that a doctor ought to be called. Then his sister's husband, who had brought him to the place, said: "God who has chased away the evil spirit, is able by the prayers of his saints to restore his sight." Then he put back, as best he could, the drooping and hanging eye to its place, and bound it up with a handkerchief, which he considered ought not to be untied for a week. That was done, and at the end of the week he found the eye quite healthy. There were other cures there also, which it would take me too long to relate.

Miracles IX, X.—I know of a maiden at Hippo, who was presently rid of an evil spirit upon anointing herself with the oil which a priest had blessed and had mingled his tears with the blessing. I know also a bishop,[1] who prayed once for a young man whom he did not see, and the young man was immediately delivered from an evil spirit.

Miracle XI.—There was an old man, Florentius, a native of our Hippo, a religious man and poor, who gained his livelihood by the art of a tailor. He had lost his mantle (*casulam*), and had not the means of buying another. He came to the Twenty Martyrs, whose Memorial is much frequented in our city, and in a loud voice prayed for a garment to cover him. Some scoffing youths, who happened to be about, heard him, and mobbed him as he went away, crying out that he had been asking the Martyrs for fifty pence to buy a coat. He walked on without saying anything, and saw cast out on the beach a large fish, gasping. With the support and help of these youths he laid hold of it, and finally sold it at a cookshop for three hundred pence to a cook named Catosus, a good Christian, telling him how the thing happened. His plan was to buy wool with the money, that his wife might make him a garment as best she could. But the cook, cutting open the fish, found a gold ring in its stomach; and presently, moved with pity and religious awe, he gave it back to the man, saying, "See how the Twenty Martyrs have clothed you."

Miracle XII.—At the Tibilitan Waters the Bishop Praejectus was carrying the relics of the glorious martyr Stephen. There came to his Memorial a concourse and gathering of a great multitude. There a blind woman begged to be led to the bishop carrying the sacred treasure; she gave in the flowers that she carried, received them back, put them to her eyes, and forthwith saw. To the amazement of those present she went before them, exulting, hurrying along, and no longer seeking anyone to show her the way.

Miracle XIII.—A Memorial of the said martyr is set up in the village of Sinita, which is near the colony of Hippo. Lucillus, the bishop of the place, was carrying the relics, the people going before and coming after. He had long been suffering from a fistula, and was at the time awaiting the hand of a surgeon, an intimate of his house, to operate upon it. By the bearing of that pious burden the fistula was suddenly healed, for he found it no more on his body.

[1] Probably himself.

Miracles XIV, XV.—Eucharius is a priest from Spain. He lives at Calama. He was suffering from a disease of long-standing, the stone; and was cured by the Memorial of the aforesaid martyr, which the Bishop Possidius had set up there. The same Eucharius was afterwards laid out for dead, of another disease. Already his thumbs were being tied together, when by the aid of the martyr above mentioned he was raised up, by the bringing back from the Memorial and laying upon his body his own priest's tunic.

Miracle XVI.—There was in that town a man, a leading member of his guild, named Martial, well on in years, having a great abhorrence for Christianity. He had, however, a daughter, who was a believer, and a son-in-law baptised the same year. When he was ill, they begged him with many flowing tears to become a Christian, but he absolutely refused, and drove them away in a storm of indignation. His son-in-law thought it the best thing to do to go to the Memorial of St Stephen, and there pray for him all he could, that God would give him a right mind not to put off believing in Christ. This he did with extraordinary groaning and weeping and a sincere and ardent piety. In leaving he took some of the flowers that came to his hand from the altar, and, it now being night, he put them at the sick man's head; then they went to sleep. But lo, before dawn, the sick man cries out for them to run to the Bishop, who then happened to be staying with me at Hippo. Hearing that he was absent, he asked for the priests to come. They came, he said that he believed, and, to the admiration and joy of all, he was baptised. As long as he lived, he had on his lips the words, "Christ receive my spirit," though he did not know that these had been the last words of blessed Stephen when he was stoned by the Jews. They were also his last words, for he died not long after.

Miracles XVII, XVIII.—In the same place, through the same martyr, two gouty patients were cured, one a citizen, the other a stranger. The citizen was cured altogether: the stranger had a revelation what remedy to apply when the pain came on; he heard, and on his acting accordingly the pain at once stopped.

Miracle XIX.—Andurus is the name of a farm where there is a church, and in the church a shrine of Stephen the martyr. A little boy was playing in a yard, when some oxen, who were drawing a vehicle, got off the track and crushed the boy with the wheel, and he at once gasped as though he would expire. His mother seized him and laid him by the said shrine, and he not only came to life, but was found unhurt.

Miracle XX.—On a neighbouring estate, which is called Caspaliana, a certain nun was ill, and her life was despaired of. Her dress was taken to the same shrine, but, before it was had back, she died. Her parents, however, covered her corpse with the dress; she recovered her breath, and was well.

Miracle XXI.—At Hippo a Syrian, named Bassus, was praying at the Memorial of the same Martyr for his daughter, who was dangerously ill; he had brought her garment there with him, when, lo, his servants rushed from the house to tell him that she was dead. They were received by his friends while he was still at prayer; and the friends bade them not tell him, lest he should lament publicly in the street. When he got home and found the house resounding with the lamentations of his family, he threw the garment of his daughter, which he had with him, over her, and she was restored to life.

Miracle XXII.—Again, also in our city, the son of a certain tax-gatherer Irenaeus fell ill and died. When the corpse was laid out, and the mourners were preparing the funeral, amid the condolences of other friends one suggested that it should be anointed with the Martyr's oil. So it was done, and the man came to life.

Miracle XXIII.—Also in our city a man of Colonel's rank, Eleusinus, placed an infant that had died of illness, upon the shrine of the Martyr that is in the suburb, and after a prayer, which he poured forth with many tears, he took up the child alive.

I am in a difficulty. My pressing engagement to complete this work puts it out of my power to relate all the miracles which I know of; and doubtless many of our people, reading this, will be offended at my omitting so many which of course come within their knowledge and mine. I now beg their forgiveness, and ask them to reflect what a long task it would be to do that which the necessity of the work I have undertaken prevents my doing. Were I to choose to leave all other miraculous cures out, and write down those only which have been wrought in the colony of Calama and ours [Hippo], I should have to compose many books; and still they could not be all collected, but only those at which written depositions have been handed in, to be read aloud in public. That is what we wished to have done, when we saw signs of divine power like those of old becoming frequent in our time. We considered that they ought not to be lost to public notice. It is not yet two years since the setting up of this Martyr's Memorial at Hippo Regius; and though to our certain knowledge many miracles have happened without written depositions being given in, those that have been given in have amounted to the number of nearly seventy at the time I write (A.D. 426). But at Calama, where there was a Memorial before ours, miracles are more frequent and incomparably more numerous.

Miracle XXIV.—Also at Uzalis, which is a colony near Utica, we have known many glorious miracles wrought by the same Martyr. His Memorial was set up there by Bishop Evodius, long before ours. But there is there no custom of giving in written depositions, or rather there was not, for perhaps it has started now. Petronia, a lady of high rank there, was wonderfully healed of a great and prolonged sickness, in which medical aid had entirely failed. When we were lately there, with the concurrence of the aforesaid bishop of the place, we exhorted the lady to give in a written deposition, to be read aloud to the people, and she most obediently complied.[1] She is a woman of high rank, of noble birth, married to nobility, living at Carthage. The celebrity of the city and of the person concerned allows not the matter to escape the search of enquirers. Certainly the Martyr himself, by whose intercession she was healed, believed in the Son of one who remained a virgin, believed in him who came among his disciples, the doors being shut—in short, and to this all our argument is directed, in him who ascended into heaven with the flesh in which he rose again; and therefore such great deeds are done through this Martyr, because he laid down his life for this faith. Therefore even now many miracles are wrought by the power of the same God who wrought those others of which we read. They are wrought through such agents as he wills, and in such manner as he wills; but they do not become known as those recorded in the New Testament are known, nor are they dinned into people's ears by frequent recitation, to prevent their dropping out of mind, and the memory of them becoming, so to say, silted up. Even where care is taken, as it has begun to be taken with us now, to have the writers' depositions of the persons so benefited read aloud to the

[1] I here omit twenty-two lines, not very intelligible, nor perhaps very pertinent. St Augustine does not further describe the cure.

congregation, those present hear it only once, many are not present; even of those who have been present few keep in mind what they have heard some days ago; and scarce anyone is found to be at the pains of telling what he has heard to another who he knows was not there.

Miracle XXV.[1]—There was one miracle wrought amongst us, not greater than those that I have related, but so notorious and striking that I should think there is no inhabitant of Hippo who has not either seen or heard of it, or can ever in any way have forgotten it. There was a family of ten, seven brothers and three sisters,[2] from Caesarea in Cappadocia, holding no mean position among their fellow-citizens. Their mother, left a widow by their father's death, was extremely provoked by some injury received from them and called down upon them a curse. The curse took effect, and the punishment inflicted on them from heaven was that all of them were seized with a horrible trembling of their limbs. In this hideous plight, unable to bear the gaze of their fellow-citizens, they determined to go anywhere they could, and wandered nearly all over the Roman world. Two of them came to us, a brother and sister, Paul and Palladia, already known by the fame of their misery in many other places. They came about a fortnight before Easter, and daily frequented the church, and therein the Memorial Shrine of the glorious Stephen, praying that God would now be appeased in their regard, and restore them to their former health. There and wherever they went, they drew the eyes of the whole town upon them. Some who had seen them elsewhere, and knew the cause of their trembling, took occasion to inform others. Easter Day came, and that very Sunday morning, when a great crowd of people was present, the same youth was praying, holding fast to the rails where the Shrine stood, when suddenly he fell prostrate, and lay just as though he were asleep, not, however, trembling, as he used to do even when asleep. The spectators were out of themselves, some with fear, some with grief; some wished to rouse him, others said no, it were better to wait and see what would come of it. And, lo, he arose, and trembled no more, because he was healed, and he stood a sound man,

[1] The *libellus*, or written deposition, of Paul, the subject of this miracle, addressed to Bishop Augustine, was read by him to his flock, and may be seen in full in his Sermon 322, tom. v.

[2] The Latin is curious, *decem fratres, quorum septem sunt mares, tres feminae.*

meeting the gaze of the beholders. Who then could keep himself from the praises of God? The church was filled in every direction with cries of congratulation. Then they ran to me, where I was sitting, ready to come out in procession. One rushes in upon me after another, the later comer always telling for fresh news what the earlier had said already. I was rejoicing and mentally returning thanks to God, when the subject of the cure himself comes in with much company; he bows to my knees, he is raised up to my embrace. We come out in procession before the people; the church was full; it rang with cries of joy, "Thanks be to God," "Praise be to God"; no one was silent, there were cries on all sides. I saluted the people, and they began again, crying in still more fervid accents. At last silence was obtained, and the usual lessons of the divine Scriptures were read. When it came to the place of my sermon, I said a few words suitable to the season and to the festive joy of the occasion. I chose rather to allow them, not to hear it of me, but to mark for themselves what I may call the eloquence of God in a work of God. The man dined with us, and diligently related to us the whole history of his own, his mother's and his brother's calamity. Accordingly, the next day [Easter Monday], after the sermon, I promised that his written deposition should be read to the people on the morrow. This was done accordingly on the third day after Easter Sunday; and during the reading of their deposition I made both brother and sister (*ambos fratres*) stand on the steps of the apse (*exedrae*) at the top of which I spoke. All the people of both sexes had their eyes on the brother standing without any unsightly trembling, while the sister shook in all her limbs. And they who had not seen the brother, nor had ocular evidence of the work of divine mercy wrought upon him, were able to see it in his sister. They saw what was matter of congratulation in the one, and matter of prayer in the other. Meanwhile, when their deposition had been read, I bade them withdraw from the sight of the people; and I began to discourse on the whole case in some detail, when, lo, as I was discoursing, other cries of fresh congratulation are heard from the Martyr's Memorial. My audience turned round in that direction, and began to flock thither. When the woman had come down from the steps on which she stood, she had proceeded to pray at the shrine of the holy Martyr. As soon as she touched the rails, she fell like her brother asleep, and rose cured. While then we were enquiring what had happened, and whence this joyful noise had arisen, they came into the basilica where we were, escorting her, healthy and sound, from the Martyr's place.[1] Then such a cry of wonder arose from both sexes, that any continuous utterance was choked with tears, and seemed impossible to finish. She was brought to the place where a little before she had stood trembling. The people exulted in her being made like her brother, as they had grieved over her remaining unlike him, Their prayers had not yet been poured forth on her behalf. but they perceived that their previous intention of praying had been heard, and that so swiftly. They exulted to the praise of God in inarticulate cries, such a din as our ears could scarce endure. What was in their exulting hearts but the faith of Christ, for which Stephen's blood was shed ?

[1] The Memorial then stood somewhere outside the church, in the precincts.

www.ingramcontent.com/pod-product-compliance
Lightning Source LLC
LaVergne TN
LVHW020642100826
845148LV00012B/2294